# Sophia and Daughters Revisited

*Reflections on Women
of Biblical Connection*

## Rosalie Sugrue

Philip
Garside
Publishing Ltd.

Revised and expanded 2019

Print-on-demand edition
ISBN 978-1-07-956421-1

Philip Garside Publishing Ltd
PO Box 17160
Wellington 6147
New Zealand

books@pgpl.co.nz — www.pgpl.co.nz

eBook editions also available.

# Contents

Introduction ...........................................................7
Prayer for Women.......................................................9

**Spiritual Women**....................................................**11**
Sophia................................................................ 12
Sarah................................................................. 13
Miriam................................................................ 15
Mahlah & Sisters ..................................................... 17
Hannah................................................................ 19
    Prayer for a Newborn ...................................... 21
Abigail .............................................................. 22
Esther................................................................ 25
    A Brief Reflection on Esther .............................. 28
An Unknown Wife....................................................... 29
Priscilla............................................................. 32
Eunice ............................................................... 34
    Prayer ................................................... 36

**Spirited Women** ....................................................**37**
Eve and the Snake .................................................... 38
Rebekah............................................................... 41
Rahab................................................................. 43
Achsah................................................................ 49
Deborah............................................................... 51
    Background to the Book of Judges .......................... 53
Wife of Manoah ....................................................... 54
The Medium at Endor .................................................. 57
Bathsheba............................................................. 59
Jezebel............................................................... 62
Vashti................................................................ 64
The Canaanite Woman — A Reflection.................................... 69
Martha................................................................ 73

**Dispirited Women** ..................................................**75**
Dinah • Tamar......................................................... 76
    *The League of Lilith* — An extract ...................... 76
Naomi................................................................. 80
      Naomi and Ruth ...................................... 82
Michal................................................................ 83
    References for Michal's story ............................. 87

**Spirit Filled Women**................................................................**88**

  Hagar ........................................................................... 89

    God Who Sees ......................................................... 93

  Leah ............................................................................ 94

  Jephthah's Daughter.................................................... 97

    Jephthah .................................................................. 97

    Jephthah's Wife ....................................................... 98

    Jephthah's Daughter ............................................... 99

  The Little Hebrew Maid ............................................ 101

  Elizabeth.................................................................... 103

  Anna ........................................................................... 105

  A Woman at the Synagogue....................................... 106

  A Woman of the Streets ............................................. 108

  Joanna........................................................................ 110

    Garden Blessing...................................................... 111

  Lydia ......................................................................... 112

**Other Notable People** ...............................................**114**

  Oded ......................................................................... 115

  Argula von Grumbach (1492–1554)...........................117

  Susanna Wesley (1669–1742) ....................................119

    Susanna (Annesley) Wesley – timeline… ................. 120

    One of Susanna's Prayers........................................ 126

  Lenna Button (1901-1940) ........................................127

  Ann Turner (1798–1893)...........................................132

  Bible Queens and Kings ............................................ 136

    The United Kingdom ............................................. 136

    Other Bible Queens................................................ 140

    Other women of royal connection........................... 140

  Alphabet of Bible Women.......................................... 141

  Alphabet of Bible Men.............................................. 142

  Bible names in Māori ................................................ 143

  Bible names in latter days ......................................... 144

**Additional Resources**...............................................**149**

  Resources with a Female Focus.................................. 150

    Presenting Woman Story Reflections in Church ....... 150

    Hymn suggestions .................................................. 151

  For study groups ....................................................... 151

    Meeting Bible Women ............................................ 151

    A study resource – 65 Female References.................. 151

    In-depth Encounters.............................................. 153

    Females Filed for Fun ............................................. 154

The Book of Ruth ................................................................ 155
Bible Parents and Children ................................................ 155
    Genesis References ...................................................... 155
Parents of Mary the Mother of Jesus ................................ 158
Seasonal Liturgies, Prayers and Reflections ...................... 160
    Advent ......................................................................... 160
    Angels for Children .................................................... 160
    Angel prayer for children ............................................ 161
    Make a sparkling Angel .............................................. 161
        Preparation: ........................................................... 161
    Christmas Intercession ............................................... 162
    Prayer of Intercession ................................................. 163
    Journeys ...................................................................... 164
    A Blessing for the Journey .......................................... 164
    Easter Leaves .............................................................. 165
    Palms for Holy Week .................................................. 166
    Prayer for Mothers and Others ................................... 167
    Queen's Birthday ........................................................ 168
        A fitting time to reflect on Queens in Scripture ..... 168
    An Acrostic Psalm ...................................................... 169
    A Winter's Day Retreat ............................................... 170
    A Prayer of Approach for Bible Sunday ...................... 171
    A Prayer of Determination ......................................... 171
    April (2019) ................................................................ 172
    General intercession ................................................... 174
    House Blessing Ritual ................................................. 175
        A Candle Ritual ..................................................... 175
        Concluding Blessings ............................................. 176
    A Liturgy for All, Regardless of Label ........................ 176
        Call to worship ....................................................... 176
        Prayer of approach ................................................. 176
        Offering .................................................................. 177
        Prayer of intercession ............................................. 177
        Affirmation ............................................................ 178
        A Commission ....................................................... 179
    Reflecting on Stories and Aging .................................. 179
        Kapiti Island – A Prayer for Simple Pleasures ......... 180
        Prayer of Approach ................................................ 181
        Offertory for Spring ............................................... 182
        Commission ........................................................... 182
    Song: Let there be peace on earth ............................... 183

Where is Wisdom?................................................................. 183
Our Holy Book...................................................................... 184
A Seed is a Promise.............................................................. 184
    Call to worship.............................................................. 184
    Discuss with the person next to you:............................ 184
    Contribute ...................................................................... 185
    Concluding words .......................................................... 185
    Prayer ............................................................................. 185
Prayer: Breath of the Spirit.................................................. 185
Eve......................................................................................... 186
References & Acknowledgements........................................ 188
Index of Women Named in this Book ................................ 189
    Handy References for Special Occasions ..................... 193
About the Author.................................................................. 194
    Also by Rosalie Sugrue
    Published by Philip Garside Publishing Ltd...................... 195

# Introduction

You may be wondering why in 2019, revise a book published in 2013, or what motivation produced this rather unusual book in the first place? I would not have raised such questions had they not been put to me by my publisher.

*Sophia & Daughters* has been out of print for five years and copies have been requested. Why then revise the text? One factor being I've written many thousands of words since 2013 – sermons, prayers, devotions, lectures and novels. Writing stimulates ideas and good ideas need sharing. *Sophia & Daughters*, though written with worship leaders in mind, consist primarily of mediations for personal use.

My recent books have focussed on resourcing leaders. *Theme Scheme* offers activities and practical tips for people working with children, youth or seniors. *Ten Plays* relates to the liturgical year providing short easy drams for churches. *Lay Breaching Basics* gives information on everything lay worship leaders need to know. As these were compiled as a resource set it seemed sensible to add *Sophia & Daughter Revised* to the set.

*Sophia and Daughter Revised* contains additional stories of Bible women and others. Some of the original *Sophia* prayers are repeated in *Lay Preaching Basics*. These have been replaced with new prayers. A new section has been added comprising of lists and notes complied as a personal resource for preparing Bible puzzles and study group material.

To address motivation requires tracking to Hokitika in the 1970s. My husband was an enthusiastic Jaycee – a leadership training group for men under 40 keen to participate in community service. Jaycees' wives were encouraged to be Jayceettes and have occasional social evenings in each other's homes but mostly to provide refreshments for the men working on community projects. Jaycee Conferences attracted hundreds of young adults.

While the men discussed important business, the ladies were entertained but we did hear the Jaycee Creed recited frequently, beginning: *We believe that faith in God gives meaning and purpose to human life* ... and ending *that service to humankind is the best work of life.* Some women got to thinking such beliefs are not a male prerogative and why shouldn't women join in the leadership training, regional debates and local projects? Hokitika Jaycees disbanded Jayceettes and gave women full membership rights. Much work went into convincing the entire county.

I also belonged to Hokitika Young Wives made up of Anglicans, Presbyterians and Methodists. We took turns leading creative monthly programmes. Some of us disliked being in a group that defined membership by marital status and advocated a name change. Community Women thrived (until many of its founders were grandmothers). A discussion on Bible characters disclosed that buzz groups could easily name 10 males, but none could name 10 female characters. Being a teacher by profession and inclination I devised crosswords and word-searches to remedy this knowledge gap.

As a motellier in Dunedin I was able to attend some courses at Knox Theological College including *Using New Zealand Short Stories as a Pastoral Resource* and *Women in Biblical Text* that led me to read beneath the text and flesh out flat, female characters. As a lay preacher I used my stories in church. They were well received. Good ideas should be shared.

*Rosalie Sugrue, July 2019*

Hats that made Heads Turn – 32nd national Jaycee convention in Dunedin, Rosalie and Jack Sugrue of Hokitika
*Otago Daily Times, 18 October 1975*

# Prayer for Women

Earth Mother, Sky Father, Creator and Sustainer of us all;
We acknowledge you as The One who prompts us to reflect.
Today we reflect on your goodness experienced through womankind.
We remember before you women who have touched our lives…
**For such women we say Thank You.**

We bring names from the past into conscious memory.
From the web of women that glisten in our family tree we silently name –
mothers, grandmothers, sisters, aunts, cousins
and others we claim as family…
Whether they live in this world or the next
we know all are known to you…
**God bless our kinswomen.**

From the tapestry of significant women who have enhanced our lives
We silently name: teachers, preachers, leaders, mentors and friends…
We give thanks for the rich fabric
woven by poets, authors, artists, actors,
dancers, musicians, craftswomen and all who inspire and influence.
**God bless inspirational women.**

For the hidden skeleton of women who work to change
attitudes and laws in the cause of justice we give thanks.
We remember those who facilitate behind the scenes,
and those who work at the raw edge of human need…
**God bless caring women.**

We have been enriched by encountering women
who persevere, endure, nurture and support;
Women of patience, prayer and charisma;
Passionate women, practical women, and fun folk…
**God Bless nurturing women**

From the intuitive nature of woman comes an urge for peace;
We give thanks for this gift and celebrate its application
be it with sibling toddlers, fractious friends or paying clients,
be it by swift action, or hard wrought in boardrooms and chambers;
**God bless peace-active women.**

From the sparkling spread of history-makers,
women we have never met but whose names and deeds
are notched in our memories as heroes and role-models;
We bring names and recall deeds and marvel...
**God bless special women.**

For the vast network of workers who keep society functioning:
business-women, home-makers, lawyers, vets,
assistants, doctors, nurses,
trades-women, seasonal workers, waitresses,
factory workers, motelliers,
presbyters, receptionists, cleaners, clerks, carers, politicians,
CEOs and volunteers ...
**God bless working women.**

For the myriad of unremarkable women:
Struggling women, suffering women, and ourselves we pray...
Strengthen our sisterhood as together we work for a better world;
Show us how to become more like the woman we admire.
**God bless ordinary women.**

Enable us to claim the best in feminist values and feminine wisdom;
Help us reveal the Spiritual within the Material,
and the Sacred within the Secular.
With strong threads from the past
and rays of bright hope for the future,
Help us weave a faith suitable for today – a mantle worthy of
tomorrow's daughters.
**God bless us all. Amen**

# Spiritual Women

Sophia • Sarah • Miriam • Mahlah and Sisters • Hannah
Abigail • Esther • An Unknown Wife • Priscilla • Eunice

*Breath of the Spirit come blow among us
fill and inspire us, with life-giving joy.*

# Sophia

I am Wisdom, as old as time and as fresh as tomorrow,
I rippled the waters when the earth was without form,
I am the inseparable feminine companion of the Creator,
With the breath of life I entered the human being;
**WE are the God who rejoices when all was good.**

I am Pentecost, vibrant as fire and as strong as words,
I am as invisible as the wind and as powerful as Love,
I am everywhere and nowhere, my nature is nurture,
Looking will not find me – I am discerned by hearing;
**WE are the God who rejoices when all will be good.**

I am as Ruah, the indefinable breath of God,
I whisper in the minds of the newborn,
I prime the soul and nudge the conscience,
I invoke the awe that prompts human response;
**WE are the God who rejoices when all is good.**

> *Then God said, "Let us make humankind in our image,*
> *according to our likeness..." Genesis, 1:26*
> *...and indeed it was very good. Genesis, 1:31*

# Sarah

We bring names from the past into conscious memory.
From the web of women that glisten in our family tree we silently name –
mothers, grandmothers, sisters, aunts, cousins
and others we claim as family
Whether they live in this world or the next
we know all are known to you…
**God bless our kinswomen.**

Yes, I laughed. Men, three of them, appear from nowhere looking for hospitality. As if we don't always look after strangers! They didn't have to spin fortune-telling yarns to get a bite to eat. These three men put Abraham in a right state. He comes rushing into the tent shouting to me to make cakes from fine meal before running off to the cowhand to order veal and get fresh butter.

When all was ready Abraham served them himself under the shade of the oak tree outside our tent. He didn't even sit with them, just stood there trying to look humble, not something he does well. I was watching from the tent door and could hear everything. They asked after me and then told old Abie I would give him a son next spring. Well, who wouldn't laugh, I am menopausal! Those men had barely set eyes on me. Actually, I don't look too bad for my age – not having children has its compensations! Abraham keeps trying I'll give him that, but me have a baby!

Abie has always had this notion he is going to be the father of a great nation. Well, you can't father a nation without the help of a mother! If he hadn't tried to pass me off as his sister and lend me to the Pharaoh for his own political safety and personal gain, this curse would not have befallen me. He couldn't get his head around the fact that the Pharaoh's court was cursed because of him.

Soon after that unpleasant incident he stops calling me Sarai, the name my father gave me, and starts calling me Sarah, which means princess. I thought it rather sweet of him, but he said it was God's command, and I was not to call him Abram but Abraham, father of many. He was so set on fulfilling his new name I became depressed and said he could try with my personal maid Hagar. She had come with me from the Pharaoh's court and was mine, a sort of extension of me. I thought it likely that she would also be cursed but Hagar became pregnant. Then she started looking down on me. I had to send her away. However, she came back with stories of an angel! And she produced a son. It wasn't easy for me. I felt cheated. But I love Abraham and want him to be happy. I thought I had come to terms with it and was trying to be happy for them. Cute as he is, watching Ishmael thrive from babe to toddler was a painful reminder of my lack. I avoided them when I felt down. As mistress of this household I have important responsibilities. I know my husband loves me dearly. I determined not to let an Egyptian slave girl upset my confidence.

Then these chaps arrive and get my Abraham all excited, yet again! I got quite a dressing down for laughing. Our God can do anything said Abraham. He was so sure I felt ashamed and tried to pretend I hadn't laughed.

Now it is spring. Unfurling leaf-buds are greening the oaks and life is wonderful. I have delivered a fine healthy son. His birth cry sounded more like a chuckle than a protest. Abraham named him Isaac, laughter. My heart is full of laughter. When the child comes off my breast his eyes search for mine and both of us smile, a deep knowing smile of connection. He is strong, he will have children of his own, even twins perhaps, and they will have children, and their children will have children... Now I can believe our descendants will be as numerous as the stars in the sky. Truly I am the mother of a nation.

*Genesis 12:10-20; 16:1-15; 18:1-15; 21:1-7*


Even in the autumn of our lives
we are in the midst of new life.

May our souls be quick to delight
and never far from love and laughter.

As we live in God's smile
so may we spread smiles in our living. Amen.

# Miriam

From the tapestry of significant women who have enhanced our lives
We silently name: teachers, preachers, leaders, mentors and friends…
We give thanks for the rich fabric
woven by poets, authors, artists, actors,
dancers, musicians, craftswomen and all who inspire and influence.
**God bless inspirational women.**

Here I sit leper an outcast, me, Miriam, – prophet, singer, dancer, and sister to Aaron and Moses. He's got too big for his sandals, has my baby brother. Does he forget if it wasn't for me, he would have died an infant? Why do men gloss over the contribution of women? He of all men should know that his life depended on women – the brave mid-wives, our mother, Jochebed, who master-minded the save-our-son plan, the Pharaoh's daughter and then Zipporah and her six sisters.

Moses may speak with God and work wonders, but he is still a man, a mortal man with lusts and temper. What right did he have to take a Cushite wife? Moses tells the people to remember who they are then lets himself get carried away by a woman who is black and beautiful. Passion has been his strength but it also his weakness. When young he felt deeply but was too quick with his fists. There is no doubting his passion for his people and his God, but Zipporah is his wife. She has borne him two sons. She too saved his life when this God business started to go to his head. Zipporah is a fine, quick-thinking woman. At times he acts as if she is dispensable. Her father Jethro was such a help in the early days when Moses was learning how to cope in the desert and turn the mob into a community.

This indiscretion is simple vanity. He wants this exotic young foreigner to prove that the years have not depleted his manhood. Aaron was as concerned as I was. He also spoke up. This angered Moses but he preferred to re-direct all his anger at me. How dare a woman speak to him in that way? Well, this woman does dare. This woman has always dared. This woman will speak up for what is right.

I was surprised that God let his curse engulf me. But I'm beginning to understand. Moses was mortified. But what was done was done. Moses had to face the consequence of his action. A great leader cannot stay great if he lacks the support of his people. I didn't ask the people to love me. I didn't know for sure that they did. But now I know. The people have refused to move until I can rejoin camp. I don't doubt that this incident will be retold and modified in the manner of tales. Male story-tellers are subtle shapers of stories, men become heroes and dubious male actions become the whim of their male God.

I looked terrible at first but whatever this skin disease is has caused no discomfort and is quickly clearing. Moses has no idea if what he did was serious, fatal even. I imagine he is quaking in his sandals. Aaron will be reciting a list of my virtues to add to his discomfort. He may even remind little brother that when we crossed the Red Sea it was I who led the people in a song of thanksgiving. It was my song, my words, my tune, my dance. The people liked the words and continued to sing it as a marching song. Before long, my song was being called the Song of Moses. He did nothing to discourage this. I didn't mind. Moses had a mighty task. Moses was the leader and needed all the help he could get. When new songs are needed the people come to me. They know I have a flair for song. And they know that God doesn't only speak through Moses.

Now the people are showing Moses they disapprove. They have discovered what it means to be a community – solidarity creates power. They bring me food and they care. I will let Moses ponder his actions for a couple more days then I will present myself to Aaron and he will declare me healed. I pray the time will come when all people of God, women and men, will be able to say with confidence and accountability 'God speaks also through us.'

*Exodus 15:1-21 & 18:1-27; Numbers 12:1-16*

# Mahlah & Sisters

For the hidden skeleton of women who work to change
attitudes and laws in the cause of justice we give thanks.
We remember those who facilitate behind the scenes,
and those who work at the raw edge of human need…
**God bless caring women.**

**Hoglah:**  You can't be serious. It's blasphemy!

**Noah:**  But it isn't right, it simply isn't right.

**Hoglah:**  The law is sacred.

**Mahlah:**  The Ten Commandments are sacred. I don't believe all the other laws are.

**Noah:**  Be careful Mahlah. What if someone heard you saying such things?

**Mahlah:**  Think about it Noah. The laws were made to protect us. If the law can't protect us the law is failing. Our mother is dead. Our father is dead. We have no brothers. We have no uncles. We are unmarried. We have 2 little sisters and there is only us to care for them.

**Hoglah:**  It wasn't easy raising five girls when our mother died but Father taught us well.

**Noah:**  He made sure we learnt the skills of the house and he taught us the skills of the land.

**Mahlah:**  He also taught us to think, to learn, to question. Is it his fault he had no sons?

**Hoglah:**  Of course not, it's just how things turned out.

**Mahlah:**  Perhaps Yahweh has a purpose for us.

**Noah:**  For us to be a family of female beggars!

**Mahlah:**  I think not.

**Hoglah:**  How else can we survive?

**Mahlah:**  How would orphan sons survive?

| | |
|---|---|
| **Noah:** | They would have inherited their fathers land. |
| **Mahlah:** | Our father has land, we are his offspring. We can work his land. |
| **Hoglah:** | But the law won't let us. |
| **Mahlah:** | What if we get the law changed? I've prayed about this and I believe it is right. We must put our case to Moses. He is a man of God. He will pray about it. Surely Yahweh will give the same answer to Moses as he gave to me. |
| **Hoglah:** | Who knows the ways of Yahweh? |
| **Mahlah:** | Yahweh is a just God. This is a justice issue. |
| **Noah:** | You're right Mahlah. Let's talk it over with the others. It is important they understand. |
| **Hoglah:** | Milcah, Tirzah, come here please. |
| **Mahlah:** | Who are we? |
| **All:** | We are the daughters of Zelophehad. We are five proud daughters. |
| **Mahlah:** | We think we should go to Moses and ask him if we can keep the land that was given to our father. We will tell Moses that we can care for sheep and grow crops. |
| **Hoglah:** | We must make Moses understand that daughters are as worthy as sons. |
| **Noah:** | How we behave is very important. How can we make a good impression? |
| **Milcah:** | We will wear our best clothes |
| **Tirzah:** | We will be very polite. |
| **Milcah:** | We will have to be very brave. |
| **Tirzah:** | We will be the Fearless Five. |
| **Mahlah:** | If we succeed, all daughters without brothers will have the right to own land. We will be blessed, and we will bring a blessing to others. Our story will be told and re-told. Not only will the name of Zelophehad be remembered so will the names of his 5 daughters. |

After praying over the issue Moses granted Zelophehad's land to his daughters, and the names Mahlah, Noah, Hoglah, Milcah and Tirzah appear in the books of Numbers and Joshua.

*Numbers 26:33; 27:1-11; 36:1-13*
*Joshua 17:3-6; 1 Chronicles 7:15*

# Hannah

We have been enriched by encountering women
who persevere, endure, nurture and support;
Women of patience, prayer and charisma;
Passionate women, practical women, and fun folk…
**God Bless nurturing women.**

Ah Little One, sweet bundle of perfection suckle to your heart's content and I will tell you a story. You know that I am the happiest of women, but once I was a sad creature. Once my lot was to be a barren wife, every day I longed for things to be different. I wondered what I had done to earn such dishonour. All my life I have worshipped Yahweh, the one true God. I tried to be a good daughter and a good wife and every day I was ridiculed by Peninnah, your father's other wife. She boasted that she had children and I had none. My breasts ached to suckle a child, but my womb remained empty. Each month I faced bitter disappointment. Sometimes it was almost too much to bear. Dark thoughts filled my mind and I could not eat. Peninnah taunted me with her brood and swaggered her proven hips at every opportunity.

Elkanah, your father and our husband, said he didn't mind that I was childless. In fact, the dear man went out of his way to assure me that I was loved, but everyone knows a woman's worth is her children. My husband may love me, but my culture does not. Maybe in some distant time this will not be how it is. Could there ever be a culture where women are valued for themselves?

One day, when Peninnah had been particularly mean, your daddy found me crying. "Why do you weep?" he asked. I was too distraught to come up with a clever answer. "Why is your heart sad?" he continued. His tenderness undid me completely. "I cannot give you a son."

"Am I not more to thee than ten sons?" he said taking me in his arms and kissing my tears away. It was not long after that we went up to the temple at Shiloh for our annual thanksgiving sacrifice. When the meat had been blessed Elkanah gave portions to Peninnah and each of her children, but to me he gave a double portion. He meant well but it made her more unbearable than ever. Now, I wonder if she was jealous of the special bond between us.

Burpy time – look over my shoulder – the woman sweeping the yard is Peninnah. See how saggy-baggy she is! Her figure has gone. Last year I didn't notice. I didn't think any woman could be jealous of a barren wife … Good boy! Now the other side, that's it. You are a quick one. You know how to find what you need. Drink well wee one. Grow strong.

I prayed every day, but God didn't seem to hear my prayer. I wondered if the Lord was avoiding our house. I determined to speak to the Lord in the temple. Surely, he would hear me in his own house. Last year when we went to Shiloh for the sacrifice I prayed as I have never prayed before. I flung myself on the ground and poured out the distress of my soul. Then a terrible thing happened. It was the most frightening experience of my life. Someone shook my shoulder and shouted at me to get up. It was the High Priest, Eli. He accused me of being drunk. "Put your wine away," he said. Oh, the shame of it! He said my lips were moving but no sound came forth. Why would I want the world to know my innermost thoughts!

But my Precious One, the very injustice of it made me bold. I told him everything and he listened. "Go in peace," he said, "May the God of Israel grant your petition." His eyes were full of kindness. Truly Eli is a man of God. I felt as if a great weight had been lifted from my soul. My whole being radiated joy. I danced to your daddy and we ate and drank and made love in our quarters. We made love many times that month, but I like to think that you, sacred child, were conceived within the holy precincts of the temple accommodation.

Before returning home, we rose early and gave our thanks. My hope was so sure that there and then I made a solemn vow. But don't you be bothering your downy head over that. You are mine until fully weaned. You and I are not even going to visit the temple for the next few years. You are a special child, a sacred gift to be offered as a Nazirite. Know from your earliest moments, son of Elkanah and Hannah, that you are blessed by the Lord of Hosts. Who knows what you may become? As an agent of the Lord you may have a hand in shaping the history of Israel. Yes, hold my finger Little One. I feel your tiny strength. It fills me with joy. You will grow into a sturdy lad.

When you are ready, I will present you to the temple. The kind priest Eli will care for you and instruct you in sacred duties. You won't be lonely. Your daddy and I will visit you every year, and each year I will make you a new set of clothes. Every stitch will be sewn with love. As my garments caress your growing limbs my love will surround you at all times. You will fulfil your sacred destiny and give us reason to be proud. Your name means asked of the Lord. Blessings on you, wee Samuel. My heart rejoices in the Lord. Our strength is in our God.

*1 Samuel 1*

## Prayer for a Newborn

Thank you, thank you, for this precious wee soul;
To help him (her) blossom is my sacred goal.
Please bless this delight that lies in my arms,
And help me proof him (her) from damaging harms.
Grant me enough patience to always care,
And the wisdom to listen, and really hear.
May this dear child laugh, and love, and grow,
And when the time comes, help me let go. Amen.

# Abigail

From the intuitive nature of woman comes an urge for peace;
We give thanks for this gift and celebrate its application
be it with sibling toddlers, fractious friends or paying clients,
be it by swift action, or hard wrought in boardrooms and chambers;
**God bless peace-active women.**

My name is Abigail. My fate was to marry a surly, bad-tempered man. My parents were pleased with the match as the man was very wealthy. 'You have been blessed with great beauty,' my father said with pride. I saw this blessing as a curse. Not only was the man much older than me his name was Nabal, which can translate to fool. My mother added words too soft for father to hear. 'You have also been blessed with great understanding.' With due ceremony (it cost my parents a fortune) I was packed off to Nabal's estate at Carmel. His livestock dotted the mount like a covering of pebbles. I was told last muster totalled three thousand sheep and one thousand goats. Despite his wealth Nabal was thick as a brick. I quickly discovered how to detect his moods and disarm his anger. Compared to many women I lived well and didn't have to resort to counting sheep to get to sleep! I enjoyed the responsibility of a large household and I was able to keep up with happenings beyond household concerns.

I grieved greatly when the prophet Samuel was buried. He was the voice of reason in the land. King Saul had become eccentric to the point it was said openly he was losing his mind, but he was not willing to give up the throne. The successor had been named, David, the giant slayer. Once a favourite of the King, David had married his younger daughter, but irrationality possessed Saul forcing David to live as a fugitive. After the death of Samuel, the fugitive chose our land to set up his camp. It was frightening witnessing the strength of the rebel army. They arrived during shearing and we were in a vulnerable position, however, we were not disturbed in any way.

One day an emissary of ten men arrived at our door. They were unarmed and greeted Nabal with flattering words. "To you who live in prosperity we bring greetings in the name of David." I served the men with food and drink. "Peace be to both of you," they said, "and peace be to your house and peace be to all that you have." I retired to let the men conduct their business, but I saw the emissary depart in haste and was filled with foreboding. My husband spoke not a word to me but never had I seen him look so smug and stubborn.

One of the young men who had witnessed the discussion came to me filled with anxiety. The visitors had promised not to harm our workers and asked only to take food for their needs. That incredibly stupid husband of mine had replied, "Who is David, who is this son of Jesse? Shall I take my bread, my water and my meat that I have killed for my shearers and give it unto men whom I know not whence they be."

I could appreciate the man's desperation in daring to tell the story. "Mistress," he said wringing his hands, "those men were good to us when we were in the fields. They protected our livestock from wolves. Do something," he implored, "No one can speak to the master. We will all be slaughtered. The army of David is 600 strong."

No one estimates numbers more accurately than shepherds! I moved with haste directing the servants to assemble food parcels. Within a short time, the asses were laden. I made a quick list: 200 loaves of bread, two large bottles of wine, five measures of parched corn, a hundred clusters of raisins and two hundred cakes of figs. The procession departed with haste, thankfully my husband was visiting a neighbour. I mounted an ass and followed the servants. My men met David's halfway down the hillside. As I came abreast David was ranting about the worthless fellow who had returned evil for good. I dismounted in haste and prostrated myself before the man of might. I begged he hear the words of his handmaiden. I apologised for my husband, explaining he was bound by folly and took the blame on myself. I urged David to accept my gifts and to take whatever he required without soiling his hands by needless shedding of blood. It was a desperate move. Women do not present before warriors without invitation.

This warrior listened to my words and asked me to stand. I looked him straight in the eye even though I was inwardly quaking. I'll never forget his words – "Blessed be the Lord God of Israel who sent you this day to meet me. Blessed be your discretion, and blessed be you, who have kept me this day from bloodguilt and from avenging myself with my own hand. Go in peace to your house, for I have harkened to your voice and to your person. I grant your petition."

I rushed back home to find Nabal feasting with a few friends. It was lucky I had not totally depleted our larder, and most fortunate that I had not touched Nabal's wine supply. The men were drinking like kings and had become very merry. Next morning, in the sober light of day, I told Nabal what had passed, and his heart died within him. With all pompousness drained he became as a dead man and after ten days he ceased even to breathe. I had dared wonder if David may offer a condolence but dismissed the thought as silly. However, in due time a messenger came but the message was not of condolence. It was a request to consider marriage. I took five of my handmaidens and gladly joined the court of David. Now, there is peace in the land, and I have born him a son, Prince Chileab.

*1 Samuel 25:1-42; 2 Samuel 3:3*

# Esther

Do you have a destiny? I believe I have fulfilled mine. True, I am Queen of Persia, but I feel everyone is born for a reason. Three years, and a lifetime ago, I was an orphan child. No, this is not a rags to riches story. As orphans go, I was lucky, my guardian was my cousin, Mordecai. He was an achiever, a man of principle, and moderate means. Mordecai cared for me as if I was his own child and gave me every advantage a girl could have. He changed my Hebrew name, Hadassah, to Esther, but never let me forget my origins. "Jews are special people," he would remind me. "Jews hold a covenant relationship with the one true God. Alas our people have sometimes forgotten what this means. We Jews were brought here as slaves, but we have risen beyond slave status. We know that God is everywhere. For three generations we have worshiped our God in a foreign land."

As I grew older Cousin Mordecai wanted me to have a good life but couldn't find any man he considered worthy of me. I was starting to get a little concerned as to my future. One day Mordecai came home quite excited. "How would you like to be a queen?" he asked. At first, I thought it was one of his little jokes – he often called me Princess. But no, the King was looking for a new wife. His senior wife, Vashti, had dared disobey him and had lost her position. Ahasuerus was looking for a replacement. The role of queen could be precarious but what role isn't? The harem offered refinement and culture. To be accepted into any royal harem is an honour and this was King Ahasuerus, son of Darius, also called Xerxes the First. Persia encompassed a massive area and the empire extended from Egypt to Greece. Cousin Mordecai was sure my beauty would grant me entry into a world of luxury. He impressed upon me that I must not reveal my Jewish origins. The more I thought about harem life the more attractive the idea became, so I mingled with the other hopefuls and duly caught the attention of the King's talent spotters.

For a full twelve months we chosen girls were pampered and painted, oiled and perfumed, fed the best of foods and gowned in rich fabrics. I admit the lifestyle suited me and I won favour with Hegai the eunuch in charge. Hegai was keen to promote me and I took care to follow his advice. When the time of preparation was complete, we would meet the king. When the King makes his invitation the harem seethes with tension and excitement, not only the women, the eunuchs get all of a flutter. They take great pride in their work! When my turn came Hegai showered me with last minute tips. That wily old bird must have known a thing or two because the King took an immediate fancy to me. Within days I was wearing the crown – the very crown Queen Vashti had refused to wear before her King. Hegai was delighted and Mordecai as proud as a father could be.

With Vashti's crown on my head I was determined to be very careful. Faithful Mordecai continued regular visits to the gate to check on my welfare. Not all eunuchs are loyal servants like my friend Hegai. On one of his visits Mordecai overheard two of them planning to assassinate the King. He bade me alert the authorities and the plan was thwarted. One always has to be on guard at court.

There was a noble called Haman, whom I disliked intensely. He specialised in throwing his weight around and belittling foreigners. However, Haman was a smooth politician and got himself promoted to King's Advisor. To make sure all knew it he ordered everyone to bow down to him. Cousin Mordecai refused saying, 'Jews bow only to God.' I knew this would not go unpunished.

Some days later, I learned to my great consternation, that Mordecai was at the gate wearing sackcloth and ashes. No one can enter the court wearing sackcloth and ashes. I sent decent clothes out to him, but he wouldn't touch them. Then I sent a eunuch to inquire as to his distress. The answer was terrible. Haman had decided to take his revenge on all Jews – men, women and children. He had talked the King into believing the Jews were dangerous infiltrators and all must be killed. Haman had sent letters in the King's name, sealed with the King's seal, to every province in the land, demanding the annihilation of every Jew on the 13th day of the 12th month, along with the plundering of their goods.

My cousin's message urged me to petition the King on behalf of all Jews. It was an impossible request. With heavy heart I replied, "Once an order is written in the King's name and signed with the King's seal it cannot be revoked."

"You must try Esther," he rejoined, "even the King's Palace will offer no protection for a Jewess. Perhaps you have come to royal dignity for just such a time as this."

No one, man or woman, is permitted to approach the King without invitation. I had not been called for in 30 days. But my friends, you know how it is – any husband can be manipulated if needs must, and this was the greatest need I could encounter. I bathed, perfumed and dressed in my best gown then lingered in the courtyard opposite the royal throne. My heart was quaking but only my eyes fluttered. After an agony of waiting Ahasuerus extended his golden sceptre towards me – the signal to enter his chamber. He asked if I had a request and I replied my desire was that he and Haman attend a feast in my apartment that evening. He accepted with an air of pleasing anticipation. That night when merry with wine he asked again if I had a request and again, I replied, "Just that you and Haman dine with me on the morrow."

I learned later, the King could not sleep that night and had asked for the record book to be read to him. He heard the entry regarding the plot to overthrow him and discovered Mordecai had not been rewarded. Next morning the King asked Haman how a fine fellow should be rewarded. Haman, and I can imagine his smugness – the man was so sure that he was the King's only favourite – suggested such a fellow should be dressed in the king's own garments, set on the King's horse and paraded through the city with the crier calling, "This is the one the King wishes to honour." The King then instructed Haman to thus treat the faithful Jew Mordecai who had thwarted an assassination plot and not been suitably rewarded. I wish I could have seen Haman's face!

However, as yet I was unaware of this conversation but very aware of a set of gallows being erected at Haman's command. That evening the King and Haman again banqueted in my quarters. Once more the King asked if I had a request. I proffered more food and wine. When both men were mellow with food and drink, I stood to make my request, "O King, if it pleases you, I began," then I flung myself at his feet and begged for my life.

My lord and master was utterly astonished. I told of the terrible law he had unwittingly passed that would mean death for all Jews, myself included. The King was furious. "Who has presumed to do this thing?" he demanded quite beside himself with fury. I replied, "A foe and an enemy." Slowly I raised my hand and pointed, "This wicked Haman." The look of terror in Haman's eyes convinced the King. Ahasuerus was so angry he stormed into the garden to recover himself.

Haman flung himself at me begging forgiveness. I remained aloof on my couch watching him grovel. Such was his distress Haman did not hear the King re-enter. The next thing he knew was a blow from the King and a terrible cry, "Will he even assault the queen in my presence, in my own house!" The cry brought the eunuchs running into the room. They grabbed Haman and covered his face. Harbona said, "Look out the window your

Majesty – see what stands in the garden of Haman's house? That structure of fifty cubits is gallows made to hang the Jew Mordecai, the very man who saved you." The King turned to Haman and spat out the words, "Hang him on that."

And so, it was done. The King called for Mordecai to come before us and I explained our relationship. Ahasuerus then took off his signet ring that he had taken from Haman and gave it to Mordecai and set him in the house of Haman.

But I could not bear the calamity that was coming to my people, so asked for further audience. When my lord raised his golden sceptre, I fell weeping at his feet and begged that he would revoke the orders of Haman. Ahasuerus replied, "An edict written in the name of the King and sealed with his ring cannot be revoked." He gathered me up tenderly and said. "You may add what you please and seal it with the King's seal." I called the royal secretaries and further scripts were written to the 127 provinces, each in their own language and despatched by fast steed. The decree stated Jews had the right to defend themselves and their property in the name of the King.

Mordecai was duly paraded in royal robes of blue and white with a golden crown of his head. The city of Susa shouted and rejoiced. It was then I knew my people were saved, and I had been born for this moment.

*Esther 1–8*

## A Brief Reflection on Esther

Esther saw herself as someone born for a purpose. Do you see yourself as someone born for a purpose? Have you ever given any thought to such a question? I hadn't until I wrote this story. I presume such a perception is not a common perception in today's world, but I do wonder if the concept is worth cultivating. Many of our worst social problems are caused by lack of self-worth.

Few of us have the potential to do something as powerful as changing the course of history. But if each person born believed they were born for a purpose, and that purpose was to achieve something good, they would be more likely to have respect for themselves and for others.

Esther sees herself born for a particular moment. In the humdrum of living many moments are mundane but all have potential and some moments become particularly meaningful. A trick of living well is to be alert to the potential might of moments. No matter who we are, noble or commoner, leader or follower, all of us have the ability to lift a mundane moment to a meaningful moment by what we do or say.

# An Unknown Wife

History gives me no name, no speech, no story. But like many unknown wives, I married an unforgotten man. His name is lauded, his word pondered, and his deeds celebrated. The impact of the unremembered is lost to the records, but we all have a story.

You may never have given me a thought, but you do know I existed. Much as I would like to tell my story in full, I am not at liberty to do so. What is written is written. All we dead can do is encourage the living to think beyond the written words to how it was for those who were there, and how their stories can intersect with yours. Oblique comments in Scripture may indicate lost people who can be found aided by research and imagination.

Come, breathe creativity into the text. You know my husband well. The Scriptures note he came from Bethsaida and his father's name was Jona. Consider Jona, why was his name remembered? Was he a successful fisherman, able to leave his elder son a fishing boat, perhaps with a proviso that he takes care of his brother?

Young Andrew was a caring lad, he noticed things, and I noticed him, but what say do women have in marriage! Simon bar-Jona was a man of action. He saw me and decided I was for him. Simon was known for his forthright manner and quick temper. But when I got to know the real Simon, I couldn't help but love him and take pride in his achievements. He bought us a house in Capernaum, near the Synagogue!

Impetuous, is the word that comes to mind for describing my husband. Simon didn't always think before he acted but his heart was in the right place. If you can't imagine us with children it may be that we weren't blessed with any, but Simon was willing to take my mother in when my father died. Mother could be demanding but I was pleased to have her company. Simon and Andrew had their world of work and male company. Men have tendency to forget about their womenfolk and take it for granted that food is ready when they arrive home.

My impetuous husband eventually became a great man, but the hero of my personal story is my mother. Without her my life would not have changed in the way it did. And without her, you would not have known that Apostles married. I take pleasure in knowing my mother is the first woman Mark mentions in his Gospel.

As you are aware, Simon and Andrew shared a fishing business with Zebedee and his sons James and John. Much to Zebedee's annoyance the four of them became more interested in listening to Jesus than fishing. They even went on tour with the preacher but on this particular Sabbath they were back in town. Most likely it was Andrew who'd warned me they would be eating at our house.

I was excited by the prospect of meeting this Jesus who had so impressed the men, and also concerned because my mother wasn't well. She had been ailing for days, and now had a high fever. It was like she was on fire, but she slept for long periods. I knew Mother wouldn't bother the guests. Simon hadn't noticed she was ill.

However, shortly after the visitors arrived, they noticed my mother. I was embarrassed but Jesus went to Mother's bed, bent over her and held her hand. Everyone stood rooted to the spot. This can't be, I was thinking, no religious man would make himself ritually unclean by touching an ill woman. And yet Jesus' action seemed holy, like he was a prophet about to anoint a deacon. I felt the Spirit of God in the room. Jesus looked into Mothers eyes and she gazed right back, then he raised her up from her bed. The fever had vanished.

I was stunned but pulled myself together and told Mother to sit down, but she wouldn't. She immediately began helping me and insisted on serving Jesus and the others.

At sundown, when the Sabbath was over, people came to our house asking for Jesus. He went outside and talked with them and healed some. When the men continued on their travels we often talked about that amazing evening.

Jesus spoke with authority yet was gracious and caring. He honoured my Simon with a special name, Peter. As for Mother she was a changed woman, still elderly of course, but happy in herself and keen to help wherever she could.

In less than three years Jesus was dead ... and so was Mother. Simon sent word for me to come to Jerusalem. I was in that upper room with those sad friends of Jesus when once again I felt the Spirit of God. This time the Spirit filled the entire house. Each of us felt we were on fire. My mother's words rang in my ears. When the momentous experience had passed our sadness had vanished. My husband was transformed, reborn a fearless leader with a mission. Simon now called Peter, immediately set about changing the world. He didn't care what happened to him but warned me it may not turn out well. I chose to accompany him. If you think this is creative conjecture, check out 1 Corinthians 9:5. During these incredible times I often thought of Mother and her words that changed my life:

"I encountered the Christ. The only meaningful response to such an encounter is to serve him and others."

*Matthew 8:14-17; Mark 1:29-34;*
*Luke 4:38-41; Acts 1:14; 1 Corinthians 9:5*

# Priscilla

For the vast network of workers who keep society functioning:
business-women, home-makers, lawyers, vets,
doctors, nurses, presbyters,
trades-women, seasonal workers, waitresses,
factory workers, motelliers,
receptionists, cleaners, clerks, carers, politicians,
CEOs and volunteers …
**God bless working women.**

My husband and I have a small business, *Aquila and Priscilla – Tentmakers* says our sign. Has quite a catchy ring about it, don't you think? Our birthplace was Pontus in Italy. We began tent-making together in Rome. When Emperor Claudius commanded all Jews to leave Rome, we set up business in Corinth. It was there we met Paul. Quite a co-incidence really – he stopped to chat as he had been a tentmaker but now calls himself an apostle. He invited us to hear him speak. We couldn't help but be impressed. He was looking for a place to stay so we invited him to our home. Quite a friendship developed, and we became believers in this new faith Christianity. It really opened our eyes as to how life could be. Paul said we were quick learners. He explained his aim of spreading the good news as afar as possible and told of his hope to establish groups of the faithful wherever he could. He intended to make Ephesus his next teaching place.

Then he put an exciting proposition to us, suggesting we could be church founders at Ephesus. We could sail with Paul and transport our tent-making to a new city. In Ephesus we would not only be business partners but partners in spreading the Gospel. This had considerable appeal. Ephesus is a leading seaport and major trading centre, the fourth largest city in the eastern Roman Empire. It is also considered a city of architecture and culture. We had heard of a gigantic amphitheatre with marble seats rumoured to seat 25,000 people. Of course, it is a pagan city but we couldn't help but be a little impressed by the magnificence of the Temple to Artemis, Greek goddess of fertility, abundance, hunting and wild life. The multi-breasted statue of

Artemis is offensive to Jewish eyes, but just to you, I will confess a sneaking admiration for the craftsmanship.

After speaking in the synagogue and arguing his faith with the Jews, Paul continued on his missionary way. God willing, he will return. As for us we work at tent-making and church growing. I must tell you about a rather embarrassing incident.

A certain Jew named Apollos, a native of Alexandria came to Ephesus to speak in the synagogue. He was an eloquent man, well versed in the Scriptures and he spoke boldly. He also began instructing the way of the Lord for he had knowledge of the baptism of John. Although he was fervent his message was not exactly accurate. I said to Aquila, "He means well, but we can't let this go on." It was a tricky situation, but it had to be faced. We didn't want to openly contradict him so waited for an opportune moment. When it came, we took Apollos aside and explained the way of God more accurately. I think we managed to make it a pleasant time of discussion and learning for despite our apprehension he appreciated our concern and listened carefully to what we had to say. I believe it is important to face up to difficulties as soon as they appear. It really helps us being a partnership, we are used to talking through our concerns be they domestic, business or faith.

*Acts 18 & 19*

# Eunice

I am mother, a Jewish mother, a good mother I hope, but just an ordinary mother. My name is Eunice. It is a good name, it means happy, victorious one. My name is not Jewish, it is Greek. I live far from Jerusalem in the province of Lyconia. My town is Lystra on highland plains of Anatolia. This plain is bordered by massive mountains to the west and south. Lystra is a small provincial city home to Jews, Greeks and Gentiles. It is an ordinary town, and like most other towns is occupied by Rome. Lystra is of no strategic importance, but one thing I will say for the Romans, is, they build roads. Roads connect us all the way from the Great Sea to our neighbouring Lyconian towns of Iconium and Derbe. My mother brought me up to be a good Jew and it didn't worry her that I married a Greek. He is a good man and my mother lives with us. She too has a Greek name, Lois, it means freed or loosened and that is how she feels living quietly in this distant place.

As I said many Jews live here and we have a synagogue. A couple of years back some travelling teachers came to our synagogue and spoke as I have never heard before. They spoke of a new prophet one they called the Christ. My mother was with me and she said this teaching is good news indeed. The teachers spoke boldly not only in the synagogue but on the streets. Crowds gathered to listen, Jews and Greeks. Whenever I could I slipped out to listen. Paul and Barnabas were different to anyone I had ever met, and I wanted to know more of the Jesus way.

One day I witnessed a truly amazing thing, this man, a beggar, had to beg for he had been crippled since birth. I'd often given him a little food and thought how blessed I am to have a healthy son. Well, Paul and Barnabas were speaking on the steps where he sits. I noticed the cripple was listening intently. Paul must have also noticed because suddenly he stopped talking and looked straight at him, then said in a loud voice, "Stand upright on your feet." And, that cripple sprang up and he walked. Well, you could have knocked me down with a feather! I've never seen the likes, nor had anyone else and soon the crowd was shouting the gods have come down in the likeness of men. They thought that Paul, being the chief speaker must be Hermes, and they called Barnabas, Zeus. The temple of Zeus is at the front of the city and the priest of the temple wanted to offer sacrifices of oxen to them and honour them with garlands of flowers. The teachers got very upset and there was a riot, incited not only by the heathen but also Jews who opposed this new teaching. I got away as quick as I could, a riot is no place for a woman alone. But I was convinced that these were good men. My mother had taken to them from the very first but I was a little more cautious, though I had suggested to young Timothy that he would do well to listen to the teaching.

When I got home, I was alarmed to discover Timmy was missing. Turns out he had heard the commotion and followed the crowd who were intent on stoning the teachers. He'd slipped among the men he knew to be followers and was able to tell us the teachers were practically unharmed. Paul noticed my Timothy and said, "Don't worry lad I worship a great God." It made a big impression on the boy. He is a thinking lad and likes to talk over matters of faith. Paul and Barnabas returned to Lystra on their return journey. They appointed elders and gave instruction for a continuing church. My boy attends with his grandmother and me. All people speak well of our boy.

And now Paul is back again with a new assistant called Silas. I hear Barnabas has sailed to Cyprus with a young man called John Mark. This good news is being spread far and wide. It is a wonderful thing. I told our Tim if he wanted to invite Paul and Silas to our house for a meal, they would be welcome.

Well, it happened! The great teacher and his companion came and ate at our house, and even my husband was impressed, said Paul was a man of the world and a talented speaker. The exciting news is Paul has really taken to our boy; I suppose he's not a boy anymore – he is a fine young man. Paul, the man of God, has asked our Timothy to consider becoming a fellow missionary with him and Silas. I know Tim has a sincere faith and it is a wonderful opportunity for him to see the world. His father is, of course, concerned, he would like his son to follow the practices of the Greeks, but he is a loving man and not very religious himself. He has always let me, and my mother keep our faith as we feel bound. He understands that a Jewish mother wants a Jewish son.

A few days after our son was born my mother said you must discuss the matter of religion with your husband. It is very important. She went on and on about it as mothers do. Timothy's father said, "When the boy is old enough, he may choose for himself." Well he has – a brave choice for an adult male. In a few days he will be well enough to travel. I feel it in my heart that this is the right thing. I may be an ordinary mother, but my boy is destined for greatness. What mother could want for more! My happiness and victory are in my son. The name Timothy means honoured by God.

*2 Timothy 1:5, also Acts 14:1-23 & 16:1-5*

Eunice and her daughter Lois lived a sincere faith that they passed to their children. Faith isn't 'taught,' faith is 'caught.' Imagine these women exampling godly lives ... see them reading the Holy Scriptures, telling the stories and modelling kindness. These are the ways that faith is caught.

## Prayer

God of our hearts and minds,
fill our souls with good thoughts,
our minds with good stories and
our hearts with sound wisdom.
Teach us how to honour tradition
While applying reason and
Experience to all Scripture
So we may be well-nurtured
To live a sincere faith. Amen.

# Spirited Women

Eve • Rebekah • Rahab • Achsah • Deborah • Wife of Manoah • Naomi
Wife of Manoah • Medium at Endor • Bathsheba • Jezebel • Vashti •
The Canaanite Woman • Martha

*Weave your deft patterns, reform and reshape us
link us together to form a new whole.*

# Eve and the Snake

A dialogue that revisits an old story.

**Eve:** I am woman. I am Eve, and somewhere throughout history there is a snake. Where are you snake?

**Snake:** I am here – slithering behind the scenes.

**Eve:** I know that voice – the voice of the serpent – the crafty snake – craftier and more cunning than any creature created by God. A voice that sounds remarkably human and benign! Snake, it is time that we had a conversation because you are behind the whole issue of man/woman relationship.

**Snake:** Is that so? Garden of Eden time is much maligned. Don't tell me you have forgotten what happened. My memory is untainted – let me remind you. After God had created the earth creature, God said, and I heard it quite clearly, "It is not good that this creature should be alone. I will make a helper for him." God produced a 'companion' in Hebrew, an 'ezer' which turned out to be you.

**Eve:** But I was not called an 'ezer' I was called an 'issa,' a woman, a wife.

**Snake:** That is true. The male creature was very keen to make that plain from the outset. The word 'ezer' was never mentioned again for you. The word 'ezer' is at times used for God elsewhere in the Bible but you were labelled woman/wife and he just as neatly renamed himself husband/man. It had nothing to do with me – I was still watching and waiting. You had little idea of anything. You could have easily stayed that way. Was that what you wanted – to live forever in ignorant innocence? I did have something to do with ending that!

**Eve:** Yes, you talked me into eating my way to social consciousness. And the result was divine punishment for all women – an eternity of dependence upon authoritative husbands? So much for the price of an apple!

**Snake:** No, no listen! I did all that sophisticated persuasion to get you out into the world where you would have a chance of understanding. I saw how things were. Being a puppet in a perfect garden was a sentence of deprivation, particularly for you. The man creature named the animals and tilled the garden. You had no function, yet you were shaped as partner – the text gatherers and editors kept that detail in their final copy. They understood the Divine intention, even though they cleverly added poetic observations about the present state of existence and suggested they were punishments. The editors were males of their time! The real price of the apple is living and knowing God's plan has been subverted. That is your problem, not mine.

**Eve:** How can I trust you? Your plan backfired. Taking that apple was charged to me as sin.

**Snake:** God's plans pose problems for those who benefit from the status quo. I've been slithering and sliding on the fringe of conversations for centuries – I've heard them all. I know what happened to the Genesis myth – Adam was not deceived, but the woman was deceived and became a transgressor (1 Timothy 2:14). The fall of humankind was caused by a woman. He lacked initiative but was a willing enough player.

**Eve:** But I am kept in a lesser role directly, or indirectly, by a crafty textual snake. You might notice that you're not the one blamed!

**Snake:** Or credited with your becoming wise! I arranged it so that you would have the gift of knowledge. I accept that I may have forced the issue before you were ready. But it is up to you to understand that images and their interpretations emerge from their own social contexts and get put alongside other texts. Remember the great affirmation of Genesis 1, male and female were created in the image of God – and blessed together. This comes before our story in the canon.

**Eve:** My difficulty is being caught in a multitude of differing understandings. How to view the ancient stories; how men view women; how women see women? So many concepts are tainted by Eve the deceiver, the woman responsible for 'Sin' with a capital S?

**Snake:** But there is another way. I showed you the path to understanding. It is up to you to claim your God intended place as partner.

**Eve:**   I am Eve, woman of initiative and resourcefulness – Eve the wise apple-eater!

*Adapted, with permission – Eve Revisits the Snake*
*by Dr Judith McKinlay – 'Women's Voice' March 1996.*

# Rebekah

Who is Rebekah? The text tells us she is the daughter of Bethuel. So? Well, Bethuel is a son of Nahor and Milcah. And this Nahor happens to be a brother of Abraham. So, Rebekah is therefore, a grandniece of Abraham – the Patriarch intent on finding a suitable wife for his son.

Rebekah is described as a beautiful young woman. Women in stories are usually described thus, but the reader can discern more than this. We know she confident – recites her lineage with pride; she is hospitable and practical – gives the stranger a drink, waters his camels, and gives assurance that he and his party would be welcome to stop-over. Her family has sufficient accommodation for the men and fodder for the camels. She accepts the stranger's gifts without fear then runs to prepare her mother's household for company. Why her mother's? Presumably because it is women who do the providing of hospitality and probably Rebekah lives with her mother, as may her brother, for it is her brother who runs to meet the visitors and cares for their immediate needs. The obliging young man is none other than Laban, who later becomes father-in-law to Rebekah's son. But that's another story.

When settled in the stranger tells his story and there is a big catch up of family news and gifts are exchanged. How is young Rebekah feeling? She must have known something big was up by the first intent stares of the visiting men followed by the gifts of jewellery. During the family news session Rebekah finds herself betrothed. Father and brother consent to what they perceive as God's will and further gifts are exchanged. Next day Abraham's servant asks to take her back with him immediately. Rebekah's mother and brother feel things are moving too fast and suggest the visitors stay for 10 days. But, the wife-broker, delighted in having struck gold, is keen to be on his way. Mother and brother then do something that surprises the reader, they say, "Let's ask the girl, she can answer for herself." Rebekah's reply is the first record of a woman saying, "I will."

Rebekah has processed a lot of thinking. She is agreeing to marry a kinsman whom she has never met, travelling a long distance with strangers, knowing she would probably never see her family again. It is a big ask! Is she comforted by the fact that Abraham's servant is convinced that God is with him and this match is of God? Bethuel and Laban are convinced God is part of the equation. "The thing is of God," they said, "We cannot make comment."

It was a massive leap of trust for the whole family. It is likely Rebekah was a young teen. Her trusted nurse was still living and able to ride a camel. This must have been a comfort to all. Not only did her nurse accompany her, Rebekah was able to take her maids, possibly 2 or 3 servant girls. It was just as traumatic for them, but the feelings of servants are seldom considered. Rebekah's family farewelled her with words of blessing and extravagant male wishes, "Our sister, be the mother of thousands of ten thousands; and may your descendants possess the gate of those who hate them." Hopefully Rebekah was cheered by the words and did not dwell their meaning. Ritual words are devised to comfort but often the phrases do not stand well in the light of scrutiny.

The chapter ends with pure romance, Isaac taking an evening walk in the fields sights the camel train. When Rebekah sights him she slips off her camel, runs up to the head servant and asks, "Who is that?" The servant replies it is my master. Rebekah swiftly covers her face with a veil. The servant makes the introductions and Isaac takes her to his mother's tent. We are told Rebekah becomes his wife and loves her. It is not clear if Sarah was at the wedding for she died soon after. The chapter concludes with '… and so Isaac was comforted after his mother's death.'

Genesis 24 is a touching family tale of faith, trust and love. All families experience dramas in wanting what is best for their children. Although the setting of this tale is far removed from our time and culture, we can relate to the feelings glimpsed beneath the text. Every marriage marks changed relationships that extend beyond the bridal couple. All marriages hold elements of misgiving. Marriage by nature is a step of faith. To have connection through family and religion is reassuring but cannot assure a happy-ever-after ending. Life is full of complications. There will always be things to worry about. Like Rebekah we may be called to step out in faith leaving the future in God's hands.

*Genesis 24*

# Rahab

A presentation for 2-3 people – 'Narrator' may be read by 'Zada.'

**Narrator:** I invite you to imagine Rahab standing at her window high in the wall of Jericho. She gazes across the countryside towards the distant Jordan.

**Rahab:** A sparkling new day awaits – oh for a sparkling new life. Enough of such thoughts! I am good at my job. Not many women are able to support a blind father, an ailing mother and four siblings, to say nothing of servants.

**Narrator:** A knock interrupts her thoughts.

**Rahab:** Come in Zada. I'm ready for you to braid my hair.

**Zada:** Good morning Madam Rahab, you are looking beautiful this morning.

**Rahab:** Thank you Zada. I like mornings.

**Zada:** So do I, mornings are so full of potential.

**Rahab:** You know Zada, we think alike. You are more like a sister to me than a servant. We have an affinity. Your story is not unlike my own.

**Zada:** I am eternally grateful for you accepting me and my child, but how can your story be like mine? You have a home and loving family.

| | |
|---|---|
| **Rahab:** | I too was raped, but not abandoned. I was gang raped by four of the king's soldiers. It happened about five years ago. I had been delayed in the city. It was near dark as I passed the tavern. The soldiers were addled with wine. No one heard my cries…if they did, they didn't dare do anything. It was after my father's accident. My hope had been to marry well so I could support my father's household. When my parents saw I was with child they didn't cast me out. They said they would find a way to care for the baby…but nature took care of that obstacle. Deep down I know it was for the best…but there are times I wish things were different. However, I determined I would provide for my parents and my young siblings. |
| **Zada:** | And you do so handsomely Rahab. |
| **Rahab:** | Prostitution is not the life I had expected but what options are there? I decided to do it well. |
| **Zada:** | Your reputation is second to none. |
| **Rahab:** | There is a certain irony being a marginalized woman housed within the margin of the city. It amuses me. Before I became disillusioned, I was proud to be a citizen of Jericho. I still marvel at the thickness of our walls. As a child I thought we lived in the best house in the world – a house with windows to two worlds – the bustling city and the great beyond. |
| **Zada:** | And now you capitalize on your knowledge with clientele from both sides of the wall. |
| **Rahab:** | I learn much from the idle talk of both citizens and foreigners. I make it my business to be informed. Men are amazed to discover women are more than bodies. Some men find conversation a turn on. Recent talk is disturbing. I hear the Israelites are approaching. They are nomads with an obsession. They believe their god will deliver them a fine place to occupy. Their god is rumoured to have great powers. I fear this may be true for it is said that these Hebrew people were once slaves in Egypt. They made a miraculous escape. It is claimed they passed through the waters of the Red Sea. Their god may be great, but the people are brutal. In their lust for land they plunder, murder and take no prisoners. Women, children, elderly, infants, even livestock are put to the sword in the name of Yahweh. |

| | |
|---|---|
| **Zada:** | Look Madam Rahab, dust on the horizon! It grows… |
| **Rahab:** | This dust marks no trading caravan. It extends for miles. This is a grave concern. My sources are usually reliable. That's it! Men are predictable. Hebrew men are just men. To save the city may be impossible but I may be able to save my household. |
| **Zada:** | How? What is your plan? Can I help? |
| **Rahab:** | I owe this city no loyalty. If conquest is their intention the Israelites will send spies. They need to find the lay of the city. We will do our own spying. A lookout will be stationed at the top window day and night, and I personally, will make the visitors welcome. |
| **Narrator:** | Early one evening Madam Rahab entertained two young spies from the Hebrew camp. |
| **Rahab:** | You can come down now Zada. |
| **Zada:** | The men are safely hidden on the roof. |
| **Rahab:** | We can relax the soldiers have gone. I told them two foreigners had approached but I had warned the visitors away saying the gates would close at dusk and they would be trapped. |
| **Zada:** | You are such a calm one. It amazes me how you speak with confidence to all men. How did you approach the spies? |
| **Rahab:** | It was easy – Good evening strangers. Can I be of service? You look travel weary. Why not freshen up at my house? I can offer you all you desire. My opening gambit was no different to usual and their response no different to most. Travellers appreciate home comforts. You served well Zada, supplying water, food and wine at just the right times. |
| **Zada:** | They were enchanted by you. |
| **Rahab:** | Yes, they were well pleased. Israelites are partial to theology. They were quite blown away with my understanding of their Hebrew god. |
| **Zada:** | The pounding on the door was a dreadful moment. |
| **Rahab:** | I will admit my stomach lurched. If caught with Israelites it could have gone badly for me but much worse for them. They were so petrified I was scared they wouldn't move but you did your part brilliantly hustling them into hiding. |

**Zada:** It was you who prepared the thick bundles of flax. All I did was cover the men. My heart was thumping I doubted there was time to complete the task.

**Rahab:** I provided lengthy details. Then the soldiers ran to reach the gates before they closed. As we speak, they are pursuing phantoms to the Jordan fords. But enough of this chatting, our guests have had long enough to contemplate their fate. It is bargaining time. While I'm engaged in negotiations you secure the escape rope to the beam by my window.

**Zada:** Why do you carry a scarlet cord?

**Rahab:** This is my marker. I intend to show it to our guests then hang it from my window after they depart. The purpose is to identify my window. When the Israelites attack, they will know which our house is.

**Zada:** What will become of us Madam! What about the children!

**Rahab:** Courage Zada, I have a plan. The marker inspiration came from the Israelites themselves. When their god struck down the sons of the Egyptians the Israelites marked their doorposts with blood. Thus, identified the angel of death passed over the Hebrew households. I intend death by Israelite to pass over our household.

**Narrator:** The people of Israel crossed the Jordan. The gates to the city of Jericho were bolted so none could pass in or out. The citizens of Jericho were nervous, but all was quiet in the Israelite camp. Only women could be seen attending to the needs of the people. Then one day the warriors formed into ranks. The vast company struck fear into the inhabitants of Jericho, but the Israelite army did not attack, not that day or the next or the next.

**Rahab:** This is a strange sight, Zada.

**Zada:** I've never seen stranger Madam Rahab. I think the Israelites have been wandering the desert too long. This marching is madness. They have no weapons only trumpets and rams' horns. This is the third day they have marched round the walls carrying their peculiar shrine.

**Rahab:** Each time they circuit they see our cord. Every soldier will know which house to protect.

| | |
|---|---|
| **Zada:** | Protect! These carnival clowns couldn't enter our city. They have no ropes or ladders, not even a battering-ram. See how our soldiers jest and jeer. The Israelites make no reply. When the Hebrew hordes crossed the Jordan, our soldiers were in a right tiz but now they aren't bothered enough to waste a single arrow. |
| **Rahab:** | Don't underestimate the Israelites Zada. Good fortune goes with them. When they crossed the Jordan, it stopped flowing. Rumour has it their god parted the waters of the Red Sea then drowned the pursuing Egyptians. |
| **Zada:** | But we have our strong walls! |
| **Rahab:** | What are walls to a god who can hold back waters? I understand certain numbers hold religious significance for Hebrew. We will keep count of each circuit. |
| **Narrator:** | A certain number was significant and Rahab was prepared. |
| **Rahab:** | See Zada. Things are different today. Each day they circuited once but today is the seventh day. They have been round six times and are still marching. Tell everyone to collect the bags they have packed and wait on the ground floor. You help my mother with the children, and I will lead my father. No matter what happens the entire household must stay within the house. Quickly now, take another piece of scarlet cord and secure it to the doorpost. |
| **Narrator:** | The city of Jericho fell as no city had ever fallen before and Rahab achieved a brand new life for herself and her household. |
| **Rahab:** | Come in Zada. I am rested now. Come and talk a while. |
| **Zada:** | Madam Rahab, you are a truly wonderful. This good life we now have is thanks to you. It was so terrible when the walls crashed down – such violent heaving, thumping and banging but your house stood firm in its tower. When the walls didn't crush us, I thought we had survived to be raped murdered. You could have saved just yourself, but you had bargained for the entire household. Because of your faith the spies led us all to safety. Israelites are no worse than other men, and some are much nicer. |

**Rahab:** That is so true Zada. I give thanks every day that God enabled me to meet Salmon. They say some marriages are made in Heaven. Now I believe it is so. My husband cares nothing for my past. It goes unquestioned. Salmon loves me and he is rich enough to provide for all my father's household.

**Zada:** And now you have a son. He is beautiful, and so he should be with such handsome parents. Does he have a name?

**Rahab:** I feel he is destined for great things. His name is Boaz.

**Narrator:** Boaz fulfilled his name mighty man of valour. The baby Boaz became the man of substance who married Ruth the Moabitess. The child of that union was Obed, father of Jesse, the father of King David, ancestor to Jesus of Nazareth. As for Rahab, her story was told and retold down the generations. New Testament writers describe her as a 'woman of faith.'

*Joshua 2 & 6; Matthew 1:1-6; Hebrews 11:29-31; James 2:22-26*

Note: Zada (Arabic for 'Lucky one') is a fictitious character.

# Achsah

I am Achsah (Ak-sa) daughter of Caleb. The bravery of Caleb is legendary. In his youth he was the one selected by Moses to represent the tribe of Judah in spying out the Promised Land. It was a daunting task. Ten of the chosen declared the mission impossible only my father and Joshua of Ephraim stood resolute determined that with God anything is possible. But the verdict of the ten meant all the people of Israel were doomed to wander in the wilderness for 40 years. Of that entire generation only Joshua and Caleb, were given the privilege of entering the Promised Land.

Conquering cities is a beastly business. I would have preferred to live the nomadic life I was born into, but my father said I was born to something better. He was zealous in doing what he believed to be God's will. Personally, I can't accept such a God and I wonder if our leaders have got it right. But of what account are the thoughts of a woman! A more pressing problem is the age of my father. Conquering cities is all very well for the young, but it isn't something a man can do indefinitely. My father has decided to encourage would-be conquerors. He is offering a prize to the one who takes the city of Kirathsepher. "What is the prize father?" I asked.

"Land of course," he replied, "but finding the right patch is a problem. The offer needs to be tempting." He glanced briefly in my direction then back again. It was if he was seeing me for the first time in a long while. My cheeks coloured under his gaze. "Daughter," he said at last, "I have found a prize worthy of the bravest warrior."

As you can imagine I took a keen interest in that particular battle. The victor happened to be a man I knew well – my cousin Othniel. It was more than I dared hope Othneil is an imposing figure known for his honour. I sensed that he was happy with his prize. In fact, so keen was he to have me wed he didn't bother to check out the land gift. When I saw this prize, my spirits dropped. There was plenty of land but no water. I couldn't believe the foolishness of my father. Did he really expect Othneil to settle for barren land? I hoped it was an honest mistake, but I feared my husband would think otherwise.

I had come into this marriage with delight but now only trouble stretched before me. Othneil would not suffer an insult of this magnitude. He would surely take up arms against my father. Only death could come of such a feud. Othneil was still too captivated by his first prize to notice all was not well. I had to act quickly. I told him that although I loved him dearly, I had been smitten with homesickness.

"Let me return just for a day," I begged, "I have a burning desire to speak with my parents and there are some things I need. Grant me this and I will not leave you again." "Your every wish is my desire," he replied.

I mounted my donkey and went straight to my father's field. I dismounted before him. His eyes carried the shifty look of apprehension, but his words were strong, "Daughter what is your wish?"

"Father," I replied, "I have come for a blessing. The land you gifted to my husband and myself contains no water source. Could you find it in your heart to extend the gift to land containing a spring?"

We studied each other for a long tense minute. His brow slowly smoothed. "Daughter your wish is wise. Tell your husband you can have both the upper and lower springs of Negeb."

Two springs – did the gift reflect love or guilt? "You are truly a generous father," I responded.

Family harmony prevailed, but alas the people of Israel fell into evil ways, and God allowed them to be sold into the hand Cushan-rishathaim King of Mesopotamia. When the people repented and called out for a deliverer God raised up my husband as that deliverer. Othniel defeated the King of Mesopotamia and became the first Judge over Israel. His rule of peace lasted for 40 years.

*Judges 1:12-15; 3:7-11*

# Deborah

Bless us with sufficient inspiration, initiative and confidence,
to be effective in the cause of peace. Amen.

My name is Deborah, in Hebrew it means bee. Does this imply one who is busy? One who makes a sweet substance? Or one who stings? I don't perceive these connections. In this place the name Deborah is revered as nurse and lifelong companion of Rebekah. The old Hebrew tales tell how Deborah accompanied young Rebekah when she set out on a camel train to wed cousin Isaac whom she had never met.

Nurse is how I am seen by some – a childless woman who nurtures, indeed I am known as a mother of Israel. But I am also a wife, the wife of Lappidoth and this can translate to woman of fire. I am a complex woman, blessed, or is it cursed, with the ability to see what others do not. My insights are recognised and appreciated, and thus I sit under the Palm of Deborah, sacred burial place of Rebekah's old nurse and share my insights with those seeking help. My role is Priestess and Judge.

I fear for my people; they have lost the clarity of vision that brought them to this land. They have forgotten their commitment to Yahweh. I have become nursemaid to a politically incapacitated nation. As their mother I have delivered some security to my oppressed children, but the enemies chariots threaten, and fire burns within my breast. But I have a vision for the future that calls the Israelites to break out of their victimisation.

I believe I am called to rally this nation to remind its warriors of past glories. My vision is so strong my words of courage will reshape the past in the interest of reshaping the future. This holy battle against those who worship multi-gods will restore Israel's right relationship with the One True God…

…And what was the outcome of my great vision? Well, I duly summoned the warrior leader Barak, instructed him in the words of Yahweh, and commanded him to raise up an army to defeat the chariots at the Wadi of Kishon – there is little room to manoeuvre chariots in a dry riverbed!

The man had no faith in me or our God. Barak appeared as a coward, or was his reluctance due to his commander being a woman? I may lack the standing of Moses, Joshua and Caleb but I am no coward. I have insight and strategy. I think, I see, I hear, I do! In Caleb's days the whole nation heard God's command to conquer, but now God chooses a lone woman to deliver his message. Was the arrogant Barak testing me when he said he would go only if I went with him? I mocked his hesitation, poured scorn on the timid sissy. I told him I would indeed go with him but the path he had chosen would not lead to glory. A woman, not a man, would win the glory.

And so, it came to pass, and my role was to compose and sing the victory song. Weakness should be despised, yet as I sang the words required to glorify battle, it came to me that I do not like what I have done. The mother of Sisera, the defeated leader, is not unlike me – we both urged our children to fight, and to do so we had to see the opponent as less than human. As for Jael, the woman who slew Sisera with feminine wiles and motherly cunning, she did what she did, merely to survive. My song of praise for Barak justifies the rape and pillage of victory. I sang of the spoils of war, a maiden or two for every man. I sang against the interests of all women. I betrayed all mothers. I was willing to die for Yahweh, but did I really do his will? Was my militancy misplaced?

Maybe, my story will serve to illustrate the evolving relationship of Israel and Yahweh? Israel has questioned Yahweh's authority like Barak questioned mine. The Israelites sinned in the past and they will sin in the future. When they cry to God a new deliverer is raised up. And Israelite women can be used in God's service just as Israelite men can. Under God's new leader there is victory, and peace, but only for a time... I can't help but wonder, is the dehumanising of 'the other' really Yahweh's plan? Is this the pathway to right relationships? Is it possible to become so attached to our ideas that we do things in God's name that are abhorrent to God? I feel a lot more evolving must happen before God can bring lasting peace to all.

*Judges 4 & 5*

## Background to the Book of Judges

Judges is an interesting book. It is set after the time of the great patriarchs – Abraham, Isaac and Jacob, and beyond the time of Moses and Joshua. It deals with early life in the Promised Land. The writing style is different from other Hebrew writings we know, and unique in the canon of scripture. Though it poses as history, set in a specific time, it is essentially a literary work that strings together a strand of oral history. This particular scroll uses a literary devise that denotes it a cyclic work. In other words, it follows a pattern – Israel sins, chaos reigns, Israel repents, God raises up a leader, Israel sins, chaos reigns, Israel repents etc.

The behaviour of its characters gets worse each cycle. In fact, the Book of Judges contains the ghastliest collection of stories in the Hebrew Bible and ends with incidents so hideous that the all tribes are in chaos and anarchy reigns. Its final verse reads: 'In those days there was no king in Israel; every man did what was right in his own eyes.' This leads some scholars to conclude it was written to justify Israel establishing kings and becoming a kingdom like its neighbours. Most scholars now think its final form was written much later. Like most books of the Hebrew Scriptures it is written from a male viewpoint, but despite this Judges contains more stories about women than any other Old Testament book apart from Genesis.

Women's stories appear at the book's most important junctures, and the women are not stereotyped as passive wives, each is a character, some perceived as good, some bad, some abused, some abusers. Some are named and some are not. Some names are familiar to us and some are not. Among these stories are: Achsah, the perceptive wife of the first judge; Jephthah's daughter, who was sacrificed because of his irresponsible actions; Jael, who sheltered and murdered the enemy; the practical wife of Manoah, who happened to be the mother of Samson, and of course there is the devious Delilah, Many of the women in the Book of Judges are initiators of action. By chapter four we find a woman taking the role of judge. That she does so appears to be no reason for comment by the narrator.

# Wife of Manoah

**Narrator:**  Motherhood is important in the Bible, perhaps too important? Biblical man tended to view woman primarily as sex object and baby machine, and always as a possession. Note the Bible always records the woman as being barren, that a man could be barren was not considered a possibility. Some Biblical women are identified merely by their relationship to a man. Nameless women have stories too.

**Wife:**  Life is what you make it, I say. Though married for seven years I am childless. Naturally Manoah my husband resents this, but I tell him some of Israel's most important mothers were childless for years and remind him of the stories of Sarah and Rachel. But I am Danite he says. So, what says I, of what importance is a pedigree, we all come from somewhere, and we can all be useful. Motherhood isn't everything. The Prophetess Miriam and the Judge Deborah didn't have children.

**Manoah:**  My wife gets a bit lippy at times. She knows the old stories too well. For a barren woman she is too content. She doesn't worry, just gets on with the household chores. I worry. These are bad times for the Israelites. The stories I remember are when the judges brought law and order to our land and now our people are leaderless, at the mercy of the lawless Philistines. This is a Godless land.

**Wife:**  Our people didn't respect law and order. My father told me the Israelites deserve what they have. In good time God will raise up a powerful leader. You moan away I'm off to fetch firewood.

**Narrator:**  While the woman was collecting firewood an angel of the Lord appeared to her and told her she would have a son.

**Wife**  Manoah, Manoah an amazing thing happened to me. A man of God came to me – his appearance was that of an angel. He was awe inspiring.

I didn't ask him where he came from and he didn't tell me his name, but he did tell me I would have a son. He told me not to drink strong wine or eat anything unclean for the boy would be a Nazirite, from the day he is born until the day he dies.

**Narrator:** Some men have a problem listening to women, Manoah was such as man. Instead of being delighted he wanted the news first-hand so begged God to send the messenger again.

**Manoah:** O, Lord, I pray, let the man of God whom you sent come again to us and teach us what we are to do concerning the boy.

**Wife:** I told him, but will he listen!

**Narrator:** God listened to Manoah and granted the request but not in the manner Manoah wanted.

**Wife:** Manoah, Manoah, the man of God has appeared to me again, come quickly, he may still be in the field.

**Narrator:** Manoah got up and followed his wife. The man was still there, after ascertaining that this was the man who had spoken to his wife, Manoah launched into his speech.

**Manoah:** When your word comes true, what is to be the boy's rule of life, what is he to do?

**Narrator:** The messenger chose not to repeat the details. He replied, 'Let the woman give heed to all I said to her.'

**Wife:** I am to eat well and not drink alcohol.

**Narrator:** Good advice for all pregnant women, hopefully it will catch on.

**Manoah:** Stay with us a while, let me prepare a kid in your honour. Do tell me your name.

**Narrator:** The messenger was not looking for hospitality and had no desire to continue an audience with Manoah. He suggested if Manoah wished to offer thanks to God, the traditional way was by offering a burnt sacrifice. And as for his name it was too wonderful for his ears. Manoah hastily prepared a sacrifice and offered it to 'the one who works wonders.' When the flame rose from the altar rock the angel ascended with it. Manoah and his wife flung themselves to the ground.

**Manoah:** He must have been an angel of the Lord; we shall surely die for we have seen God.

| **Wife:** | If the Lord had meant to kill us, he would not have accepted our offering or told us the things he did. |
| **Narrator:** | The woman bore a son and named him Samson. The boy grew and the Lord blessed him. The spirit of the Lord stirred within him. |

## Concluding thoughts

In many Bibles chapter 13 of Judges is subtitled *The Birth of Samson*. This little known tale has some interesting aspects. It touches on the comical with the man being presented as timid, uncomprehending and inept. The name Manoah means 'rest' and he appears a little like the peasant husband of some European folk stories. The wife is practical one who behaves well. However, the Bible text gives no glimpse of her feelings, nor is there is any mention of sex. Some commentators say this may be offering a contrast to the well documented sex life of their son.

The chapter ends with lovely lines – "The boy grew, and the Lord blessed him. The spirit of the Lord stirred within him." This mother is not unlike Mary the mother of Jesus. Both see an angel and by accepting the message say Yes to God. Jesus, Luke tells us, grew in wisdom and stature. Both mothers played their part well, but one son rises to the challenge and the other fails. This is life. Mary is called 'blessed' the other mother is not even given a name.

Most parents have high hopes for their children. Have you noticed the stirring of God in your children? It is a fine thing to observe. Not all parents and carers would describe it in these terms but most feel pride and joy as they watch their small children achieve milestones and make discoveries. Yet, despite the best of parenting intention, some children let their parents down. The most we parents can do is love our children. We are not responsible for their actions. We may be able to help them face consequences but well before childhood ends, they are their own person. We can do little more than offer opinion and continue to love them.

Chapter 14 of Judges is subtitled *Samson's Marriage*. Samson's parents expressed strong disapproval of his choice of wife but stood by him when he messed things up. Samson goes on to have more wild adventures. We are not told how his parents feel or how he feels towards them. Not all love is seen to be appreciated, but nothing is lost on the breath of God. When love is given to a child the moment is blessed. May the Spirit of the Lord continue to stir in your children, may the Spirit continue to stir in all of us.

*Judges 13:1-24; 14:1-7*

# The Medium at Endor

I did not ask for this gift. Danger lurks in all power be it possessed by man or woman. Power is thrust upon some and some earn it by deeds. Special powers are particularly dangerous. Special-sight powers are gifted, unasked. With power comes responsibility. Not all possessors of power understand this. Most of my kind are keenly aware, but those with political power are readily corrupted by its nature.

King Saul finds his power so fragile he is continually searching for any he supposes may challenge it. He has become paranoid thinking everyone is bent on deposing him. Suppression of challenge is uppermost in his mind. To this end he has forbidden all wizards and mediums from the land. We do not seek to dethrone him. Our role is to help troubled souls where we can. They come to us. We do not go looking for clients. The messages we receive are not always cheering but we are bound to speak what is visioned. Sometimes we can help resolve a past conflict and permit troubled souls to rest in peace. It is not wise to seek knowledge of the future. If glimpsed as grim it is almost impossible to alter what is predestined.

It is night. Three hooded men have sought admittance. I feel they have a request and I'm filled with unease. One speaks. He speaks with a ring of authority. "Woman," he says, "Consult a spirit for me. Bring up the one whom I name."

I remind him that what he asks is illegal. I feel he is setting a snare for me. I want nothing to do with him. I want these men gone. They have bad vibes. But he swears before the Lord and promises that no evil will befall me. His voice is filled with urgent sincerity, and I soften. I ask whom he wants brought up. He names the Prophet Samuel. The entire country has mourned the death of Samuel. He was surely a man of God. The task may be beyond me.

But no, a divine figure is coming up from the ground. An epiphany grips me. I know who my client is, and I cannot stop myself from shouting, "Why have you deceived me? You are King Saul!"

The King repeats I must not fear, just tell what I see, and it will be well with me. I describe the vision. "He appears as an old man wrapped in a robe." The King and his escorts bow to the ground. Though filled with the deepest foreboding I cannot stop what has begun. Samuel is not pleased at being disturbed. The King wants to know the future. It is bad, very bad, the worst. He and his sons will die, and his army is to be handed to the Philistines. The Prophet returns to the earth from whence he came, and the King is in a state of collapse on my floor. His extreme terror is like a faint and dreadful to witness. His attendants tell me he has not eaten for a day and a night.

This I can relieve. I offer him a portion of bread, but he refuses to eat it. However, his attendants persuade him and put him on my bed. As the King rests I slaughter my fatted calf and prepare the meat. While it is roasting, I take flour and knead it to make unleavened cakes. They eat and leave while it is still dark.

What I had visioned came to pass. The great sorrow I felt when the king fell on my floor stays with me. I wish I had not been used in this way. But it brought home to me that kings have fears as ordinary mortals fear. Oppressive laws are a product of fear and the greater the person the further they fall. This king I had hated was human and I felt compassion for him. To comfort him with food was a gift I was pleased to give. But history is unlikely to record my feelings or even my name. If I make it to the records I will be spurned as a witch, The Witch of Endor.

*1 Samuel 28:3-25*

*God of wisdom*
*Help us not to spurn what we do not understand.*
*Lead us into patience and empathy.*
*Even if we cannot understand*
*Help us to do what we can to lessen suffering. Amen.*

# Bathsheba

You know my name for you have read the sacred texts. Even if you haven't read the texts a mild interest in classical art will supply a title. In the texts and in paintings I am not a person I am an object to be viewed through male eyes. My name is Bathsheba. What image comes not you mind? Is it not a beautiful woman taking a bath?

Like most ancient texts the stories were recorded by men. The hero is the one to identify with. The hero may behave badly to add excitement to the story, but all is forgiven if there is a moral to be found. The listeners have scant concern for the people the hero meets and often destroys along the way. The supporting roles are flat characters their purpose being only to enable adventures for the hero. And so, it is with the records of the Hebrew kings. In real life flat characters do not exist. In real life all people have feelings. For King David's story to read as a morality tale it must be read through male eyes.

My first appearance in David's story is when he views me voyeuristically from the royal rooftop. I am quite unaware but what David sees is recorded and a narrator discloses intimate things about my body.

Next time I am visible in David's story the reader can no longer ogle me for I have become the king's wife. My feelings on how this happened are not recorded or considered. The heartbreak of me losing the most loving and loyal of husbands is of no concern. That I was married to the one who ordered my husband's murder is of no consequence to the record keeper. I am followed from bathing to bedding without comment. All I am permitted are three spoken words, "I am pregnant." By withholding my reactions, the narrator eliminates a route of empathy for me.

I submit to pregnancy and childbirth simply so King David can lose a son and learn a lesson. As if David doesn't have many sons. The child I bear is my first born, and I weep. Yes, you know I weep but your feelings are for the now-repentant master sinner, David. You presume I weep for the child, and I do, but I weep as much for the father who should have been, for arranged murder and forced adultery.

Yet, I know that to survive I have to put these things behind me. In life bad things happen and to dwell on the bad ruins the present. I will put my trust in the Lord. In due time we had a second son and named him, Jedidah, that means invoke Jehovah.

Do you remember Michal? Probably not until reminded she was the repressive wife who spoke out against David dancing to the Lord. Poor Michal loved with the passion and total commitment of first love. Michal and David met in the royal court as teenagers when King Saul hailed David as hero for slaying the giant. King Saul had promised his daughter's hand in marriage to any warrior who killed the giant. Did the daughters of Saul have any say in this? As we know well, story princesses normally do not. A remarkable thing about this incident is that the elder daughter wasn't interested in the youth and because young Michal was besotted, the King allowed her to be the prize. She gave her all, even to the wild extreme of going against her father to protect him. But when Michal dared comment on her husband cavorting near-naked in the streets before the sacred ark, she was silenced. Never mentioned again in the scriptures, literary murder is what we call it.

Literary murder is not my fate. In the records am allowed to develop a little character. Clothed in queenly respectability I am permitted to see, speak and act, in order to promote my second son as his father's heir. Of course, I love my son and I suppose all royal mothers imagine their royal child on the throne. My Solomon, yes, he is known as Solomon now, it means peaceful, my son wasn't a contender, though he was always a favourite of David.

The King's eldest is Adonijah. I was not surprised when Adonijah began acting as King prematurely. His mother Haggith was doing all she could to promote him. Adonijah had been well groomed for the task. I was as surprised, as I was uneasy, when the prophet Nathan suggested I feed David some half-truths. Nathan was the prophet who had caused David to repent over the death of my beloved Uriah, could he do wrong? Nathan should know the will of God.

Being the mother, I am it was easy to convince me that everyone who counts has special regard for my son. Perhaps David had suggested Solomon was the chosen one? I could at least speak to his father on the matter. And thus, I had my word with the dying king, several verses of words, in fact. And with Nathan's help David was convinced Solomon should be his heir.

Like my first appearance in the 'official record' my final appearance begins with mention of a beautiful young woman. This time the 'fair one' is the woman the attendants have chosen to 'warm' the ailing king. He does not respond. It is all recorded. Can it be the record keepers are at last sneering at David? The man famed for his potency has lost it. It isn't fair. David was great in many ways. Always larger than life was David, but he ruled well, loved with passion and repented with passion. Historians back winners.

If women were the compilers of history would life be different? I'd like to think morality tales could be found in compassion. I'd like to promote mercy and righteousness, to consider the possibility of the meek inheriting the earth, and peace-makers being blessed. But I am no longer pure, and bathing cannot make it so. I have been at court too long. Politics corrupt, I have become ambitious for my son. Where is wisdom?

*2 Samuel 11:1-26; 12: 1-25; 1 Kings 1:1-36; 1 Chronicles 3:1-9*

# Jezebel

To Hebrew historians (and most other historians) wives were not important. Very few Bible queens have a story. Regardless of the Biblical 'bad press' meted out to her, Jezebel was a woman of distinction. She was Phoenician princess, and as such worshipped Baal and his consort the goddess Ashera. Ashera was symbolised by a tree or a pole. So, by making a sacred pole, 'bad' King Ahab was accommodating his wife's religion. In human terms it could be seen as an act of love. In the understanding of those who recorded the Hebrew story Ahab's acts were blasphemy. Poetic Hebrew used metaphor. Anything but the exclusive worship of Yahweh was identified with sexual promiscuity. What began as metaphor came to be taken literally. Thus Jezebel is interpreted as a seducer, instead of a person of leadership. Her husband Ahab, though King was not a leader.

Jezebel ordered the killing of the prophets of Yahweh. From the Hebrew view this is pure evil. But, like most 'religious wars' it was more about politics than religion. The prophets of Yahweh were actively causing trouble. Being a strong ruler of the time, she saw her role as protector of her country and her faith. For all his faithfulness and bravado Elijah was not a model of religious tolerance, delighting, as he did, in slaying the 450 prophets who ate at Jezebel's table as the text puts it.

When King Ahab wanted his neighbour's vineyard and Naboth refused to sell Ahab sulked. From our point of view Jezebel's action in getting him killed was murder and clearly evil, but her brutal response is understandable if viewed as a royal reaction to insubordination, in a time unknown to democracy. Jezebel outlived Ahab and at least two of their sons.

An appreciation of Jezebel's strengths can be evidenced in her final appearance at the window from where she met her death. Is it fair to mark her as the painted woman because she used power-dressing to confront a royal enemy? Was she not appearing in the full glory of her queenship, a strong leader, defiant and royal to the end? By stark contrast her husband not only disguised himself so he wouldn't be recognised in battle, he encouraged an allied king to wear his royal attire to further divert attention from himself. But a stray arrow took Ahab down.

Ahab was succeeded by his son Ahaziah who died within two years, the throne passed to his brother Joram. Twelve years later Joram was challenged by the southern king, the usurper Jehu. "What peace can there be, so long as the many whoredoms and sorceries of your mother Jezebel continue?" he asks. Jehu then kills Joram and proceeds to Samaria, where Jezebel, with eyes painted and head, adorned confronts him from an upper window. She begins with a masterful bit of political name calling by addressing him as 'Zimri' the name of an earlier usurper famous for his assassinations. However, her own eunuchs turn on her and cast her out of the window, and she meets the death predicted by Elijah.

What is the point of the story? From our time and culture, it is impossible to say. Like all Bible stories it was not recorded for us, but none the less the Bible is 'our holy book' our resource of ancient stories, myths, poetry, semi-history, philosophy and wisdom. And throughout the Bible is a human attempt to discover a worthy God, and what such a God would require from those who claim this God as their own. The God of the Bible is an evolving God, just as our faith is an evolving faith. God may be the same, yesterday today and tomorrow, but our understanding is not. Each generation has to discover God for their time, just as all persons have to forge a faith for themselves. There is a place in our inherited folk-lore for arch villains. Calling the woman Jezebel and the man Judas fit a need. Real life is not that simple. Reading beneath the text in the Bible enables us to feel into what motivated its characters. In so doing we can see that Jezebel and Judas have both been maligned but we can also appreciate that as household names they have a mythological purpose.

*1 Kings 16:29-34; 21:1-16; 2 Kings 9:30-37*

# Vashti

Greetings in the name of the Most High, may you live long and prosper.

I am merely a servant, but you are seekers of stories that give women voice. I have some insight to the words of voiceless women and have witnessed many things ... indulgence and intrigue, treachery and treason, seduction and sedition ... indeed I could tell many stories, but you are a discerning audience. I am told you value wisdom over power and bravery over violence.

O worthy listeners, establishing rapport contains its own enlightenment. So first I will tell you a little about my humble self. My name is Harbona. I served many years in the fabulous court of King Artaxerxes the 2nd of Persia, also known as Artaxerxes the Great. This most powerful of monarchs has many names. Your scriptures name him King Ahasuerus. As for those of us who serve him our informal preference is Long Hand.

Despite being the son of a slave, my life has been one of privilege. I had ear to the affairs of state and personal confidences were sometimes shared directly to my ears. This privilege came at great cost. Never will I have a wife or children. Celibacy is a choice made by some ascetic souls, but it was not a choice made by me. The sexual minority that defines me and my kind was unwillingly imposed. Resentment lingers with malice in a few.

However, most of us who survive the physical trauma overcome personal anguish sufficiently to enjoy a better lifestyle than most born into slavery. A strong camaraderie exists between us. As for kinship we harem eunuchs cherish the women in our care as our children. In regard to our Lord and Master we are honoured to be of service.

Long Hand likes to be surrounded by young flesh, so now I share quarters with a few others of my kind. We care for the rooms and grounds of a seldom visited royal outpost, and a right bunch of fussy, old queens, we are.

But once we served in the Citadel of Susa, the winter palace of Artaxerxes the Great, the one who rules over 127 provinces from India to Ethiopia. The Citadel is a splendour to behold. It stands as a shining city on a hill. The walled complex includes aesthetic structures grouped in a pleasing manner.

The central edifice is supported on marble pillars. Its arched windows are hung with curtains made from exotic white cotton, enhanced by blue hangings and tied with cords of purple attached to silver rings. Couches of gold and silver bask invitingly on a mosaic pavement set with rock crystals and mother-of pearl. Landscaped multi-courtyard gardens display many plants and water features.

Yet for all its extravagance and luxury, life within the royal court is fraught with danger. Royal personages have a nasty habit of disposing of each other and close kin are not immune. As for lesser beings, at court one's life and status are dependent on the whims of the King. The Greeks epithet him Artaxerxes Mnemon 'memory' meaning 'he remembers.' Keeping in the King's favour is of paramount importance from slave to Queen.

The citadel's harem is large, and I have tended many women but the King's first Queen remains my favourite. Queen Vashti came from a long line Babylonian of royalty – her father being King Belshazzar, son of King Amel-Marduk, son of King Nebuchadnezzar. Vashti was a mere child when she came into my care.

The dastardly events unfolded thus. During her father's rule, the Medes and Persians attacked Belshazzar's palace in Babylon and murdered him in his sleep. Hearing a disturbance young Vashti ran to her father's quarters and was kidnapped by none other than King Darius himself. The maiden was exceedingly beautiful. Darius decided to gift his blue-blood prize to his eldest son as a fitting bride.

Vashti held her head high when presented to me for the titivating and tutoring required before meeting her husband to be. Despite her terrible losses Vashti had the bearing of a princess. Within her dark ringed eyes was the glint of rebellion. My heart went out to the brave maid, but rebellion is not a healthy emotion. I determined to do my utmost to keep this child safe. My strategy was to tread softly and begin with physical needs. Accordingly, I treated Vashti to the best of baths, massages and perfumes. I oversaw her diet and guided her choice of garments, providing options and allowing the final decisions to be hers. And thus, trust was established between us. Princess Vashti was already well versed in courtly politics and quickly grasped the subtle implications of my teachings. Beauty makes an excellent mask for intelligence. Vashti allowed her King to draw conclusions that pleased him. As for me I observed impressive political understanding.

King Darius died in the 19th year of his reign. His son, not yet 40 years of age, was crowned Artaxerxes the 2nd of Persia. In the third year of his reign Artaxerxes decided to hold a great banquet for all the nobles and governors throughout his provinces. "Be sure to invite their wives," advised Queen Vashti, "I will ensure that they are entertained in a manner that will enhance your reputation."

To me she confided that should any of the assembled nobility use the occasion for usurping attempts she would have control of a valuable group of hostages. "My Lord and King uses banqueting as a vehicle for displaying wealth and power," she explained, "I take a wider view. Eating together creates bonding that can be used for good or ill," then added with an arch smile, "Why shouldn't women feast as well as men?"

Vashti's things-to-do lists were extensive. They included accommodation plans, with attention to little things like ceramic platters and golden goblets, serving water as well as wine, along with the complex matters such as food, entertainment, and unobtrusive security.

However, I was not in attendance at the Queen's elegant banquet. As a senior eunuch and one of the King's most trusted seven, my first duty was serving him. On the seventh day of feasting when the King was merry with wine, he commanded all seven of us to stand before him. Long Hand was partial to pomp and ceremony. Mehuman, Biztha, Bigtha and Abagtha, Zethar, Carkas and I duly presented in order of height, listened to his command and exited walking backwards as protocol demanded. Out of our master's sight we dissolved into a dither of distress. Long Hand's command was that we bring Queen Vashti before him to dance. He wished to display his Queen's great beauty to his drunken guests.

It is usual for troupes of dancing girls to entertain at court. Wearing silken garments and sparkling jewels they delight with synchronised movements of great elegance. A wife does not dance for anyone except her husband. To command such a thing was shocking enough but Long Hand's instructions as to her costume was outrageous! His instructions were that the Queen appear wearing her crown ... only her crown. I exaggerate not, fair audience, never would I create such a scandalous detail for entertainment.

Your Hebrew scriptures do not make the situation clear but Jewish Midrash does. We eunuchs were in a state of high agitation but our darling Vashti remained calm. The Midrashic account explains that the request was made three times. Queen Vashti replied with sage advice, messaging that such a demand was not only immoral it was a political mistake that would go badly with him. He was in no mood to accept such advice. She refused to do his bidding. Our agitation turned to fear. Vashti reiterated that she would not agree to being exhibited as a sex object for anyone, and nor should any woman. "But you are not any woman," I pleaded. "You are a Queen, the wife of Artaxerxes the Great. He will not tolerate disobedience." As our eyes locked, I perceived a moment of sad tenderness firm into rebellion. "A wrong can only be righted if someone takes a stand. My influence is limited but as Queen I have more influence than most women. I must set an example for all my sisters, whatever their status."

When Long Hand realised his wife had disobeyed him, his shock was palpable. Rage welled like a smoking volcano, but sudden fear blocked the lava flow. Blatant disobedience was new territory for this King. We seven were abruptly dismissed, much to our relief I must confess, with the command to summon his seven sages who were well versed in laws and customs. They in their turn were greatly bothered. "This outrage must be stopped immediately," they counselled. "Your Queen may influence her guests. What of our wives, and indeed all wives? Such sedition could spread like wildfire. Right throughout the vast kingdom, women high and low alike, may cease to obey their husbands."

And so it was written, in the laws of the Medes and Persians that cannot be broken: "Vashti is never again to come before King Ataxeres; and let the king give her royal position to another who is better than she."

And thus, it came to pass. Queen Vashti was replaced and written out of the formal histories. Whether she was followed by one better than her is debatable. O attentive hearers, know this, Vashti's influence was not forgotten.

Her replacement was pleasant on the eye and a worthy contender in that her heart held goodness. But they were the only attributes young Esther shared with my Vashti. Did I tell you Vashti's name was derived from Old Persian and means 'excellent' or 'best of women'? Yes, yes, I know Esther means 'a star' but that name was bestowed as part of her makeover. The poor child was an orphan labelled with the name Myrtle – facts that were not disclosed to his Royal Highness. Not only was the maiden an innocent, she was completely lacking in noble blood and court experience. But Hegai, who was in charge of the new intake of harem hopefuls, became besotted by her. He staunchly maintained Esther was a very quick learner. That may be so, but she was of a passive disposition. Passive women are as numerous as the seeds of the pomegranate. My spirited Vashti was a golden apricot by comparison.

There is no doubting that clucky Hegai achieved wonders with his little orphan. She impressed the King, so completely winning his favour, that no questions were asked. By this time, we eunuchs had learned of another fact that we took pain-of-death care not to divulge. Though bursting with pride at Esther's success, it nearly broke Hegai's heart having to cease his lavish mothering. As Queen, Esther was attended by Hathach.

Hathach was loyal and efficient in his duties but not noted for creativity of thought. When Esther became aware of distress outside the palace she sent Hathach to enquire of the matter from her Jewish relative Mordecai who had been observed wearing sackcloth and ashes. Thus, Hathach learned of Haman's plot to kill all Jews. Confronted by Esther's terrible dilemma Hathach elicited my support and presented me as a trusted counsellor. Unexpectedly, I perceived true nobility in the Queen's distress and my mind filled with visions of her predecessor. Vashti's words came to my lips, "Eating together creates bonding that can be used for good or ill." And a plan took shape in my mind.

I supervised the intimate little feasts Esther held in her own quarters for the King and his advisor Haman. And thus, I was present when the King offered to grant his Queen any request up to half his Kingdom. I witnessed the extreme bewilderment of the King when Esther asked that her life be spared along with the lives of her people. With passionate eloquence the Queen explained her heritage and how the law to exterminate all Jews was the work of a wicked man in high office who was also plotting to murder the King.

The King was so disturbed he left the room, but not for long. He returned to find Haman on the Queen's couch begging for clemency. When that villain Haman made the pathetic plea for his life, it was I, Harbona the humble, who directed the King's eyes to the window that framed the gallows Haman had prepared for Esther's closest relative Mordecai.

Without the influence of Queen Vashti, Queen Ester's story would not have had its happy outcome. O worthy audience I ask that you remember Queen Vashti as the role-model heroine she was. May Vashti's story continue to inspire those who seek to right wrongs.

*Vasthi's story is found in Esther 1*

*Harbona's victory, Esther 7*

# The Canaanite Woman — A Reflection

Many preachers have found this story difficult. Rather than face its difficulties they have stressed the Canaanite woman's faith and humility. Congregations were encouraged to leave with the message that Jesus responded to this woman of faith by healing her daughter.

But, when faced up to, this is a much bigger story than that. It could be argued that had it not been for this incident, Christianity may not have extended beyond Palestine. Without the influence of this Canaanite woman you or I may never have heard of Jesus.

What we so often forget is that Jesus lived in a particular time and location. Jesus of Nazareth was a real person, and like people everywhere could not help but be influenced by his time and culture. In common with many famous people Jesus was 'a man ahead of his time' but, only in some things. We are all shaped by the circumstances of our upbringing. Jesus was born into a peasant family, in a culture where men did not have public dealings with women and where Jews did not have dealings with Gentiles.

In the two Gospel accounts of this incident we see Jesus as a man who has been travelling with friends, travelling long miles on foot in a hot and dusty country. He is tired, they are all tired and all they want is some peace and a chance to rest, but a certain arrogant person won't let them do what they need and desire. The intrusive person is a Gentile. We need to understand that strict religious laws prohibited inter-racial dealings but even apart from religious issues, Jews and Gentiles despised each other. But, horror of horrors this embarrassing intruder is not only a Gentile, the arrogant one is a woman. No self-respecting, decent woman of the time would approach any man in public, let alone a highly respected teacher and healer.

So, what made this woman break all the taboos of her race, class and gender? The one fact we know about her is she is a mother – a mother made bold for the well-being of her child. Mother-love can drive desperate action. This was desperate action. The woman knew she risked ridicule, rudeness, assault and worse. In this encounter she was breaking the rules of decent society. The disciples were justifiably angry. But where it gets difficult from our view-point Jesus also was angry. Despite her desperate plea he ignored her.

This is not the Jesus we know. We know a Jesus who when tired welcomes children and stops his disciples from sending then away with a clip over the ear. We know a Jesus who outrages the general public by dining with outcasts. The Jesus we know heals sinners and engages in theological discussion with men and women, regardless of race or status. But this much loved Jesus did not begin his mission with such inclusive ideals.

We 21st century citizens live in an interconnected global village – little New Zealand is dead scared of the effect that will flow onto us when the American stock-market falls, or riots break out in the UK. Life didn't used to be like this. Once everything was local, from the economy to the gods one worshipped. Village life was but a step away from the nomadic tribal lifestyle when anyone who wasn't a member of the clan was highly suspect.

Jesus was a Jew and when he began his mission, he naturally believed that he was chosen by a local God to minister to a local people. Matt 10:5 tells us of Jesus instructions to his disciples… "Go nowhere among the Gentiles and enter no town of the Samaritans but go rather to the lost sheep of the house of Israel."

Our un-named Canaanite woman had no useful family connections and no back-story for us to empathise with. Her story doesn't fit into a family saga nor run to chapters. Her Scripture appearance is but a cameo of a few verses, yet what she did was possibly as important for Christians as what Joseph did for Judaism. The Canaanite, or Syrophoenician as Mark describes her, was a nobody. Yet this particular nobody was bold and desperate, but not only bold and desperate, she was informed and intelligent.

Somehow, she had heard of the remarkable ministry of Jesus and realised if anyone could help her ill daughter it was the foreign preacher man. The woman knew she would encounter resistance but was determined that she would persist until she was heard. And persist she, did provoking Jesus to verbal anger. Even for Kiwis in a sheep country of respected working dogs, to call someone a dog is not a compliment. For a Jew to liken anyone to a dog was the worst of insults – Jews hated dogs and had no use for them considering them to be horrid unclean creatures. But Canaanites had a different attitude to dogs. The Canaanites had discovered dogs could become loyal pets and it was not unusual for them to have house dogs.

Most of us would have slunk away after getting the silent treatment from the VIP, let alone continuing to gross insult stage. This woman was made of strong stuff. She not only took the insult on the chin she answered back with a retort that was both clever and witty. Jesus was stunned. Her reply literally stopped him in his tracks and jolted him out of his pious Jewishness. The woman took the opportunity to fling herself at his feet. Jesus looked at the arrogant woman who dared make a spectacle of herself first by calling out and now holding his feet. Jesus looked and saw a person, not a despised Gentile female but a fellow human, a child of his God.

Was the woman's act of kneeling at the master's feet, an act of humility and reverence or a last ditch tactical move that showed she had shrewd understanding of theology. Jews and Gentiles shared the same scriptures. The Canaanite's were particularly fond of Jacob.

In the story of Jacob, you will recall that when he fled from his brother Esau, he had to sleep in the open using a stone for a pillow. The name of the place was Bethel. Bethel was beyond home territory. Jacob was frightened for many reasons but particularly because he thought he had gone beyond the protection of his god. He was also very tired. Stone pillows lack sleep inducing qualities but Jacob slept. His dream was not only vivid, it was an epiphany. By seeing angels descending up and down a ladder to Heaven Jacob realised God was in this place. His God had no boundaries!

Many years later Jacob decided to return home and face his brother's wrath. In this same place, Bethel, Jacob encountered a stranger who appeared to be a deity. The stranger wrestled with him all night. Jacob was injured by the stranger, but he clung to him. Having grasped the divine Jacob would not let go until a blessing was granted. There are echoes of this old story in the new one. The God-wounded woman kneels at the feet of Jesus and refuses to let go until blessed.

The woman got her blessing and her daughter was cured. But Jesus also got a blessing. The eyes of Jesus were opened to see his mission was much bigger and far more important than he had previously thought. The woman didn't keep silent about her blessing she let it be known that the God of Israel had cured her incurable daughter. After this healing great crowds came to Jesus and he was able to heal all manner of inflictions.

This woman is an inspiration. She had faith alright. She had faith in Jesus, but she also had faith in herself. Had this desperate mother not been so determined and undeterred it is possible that only the Jews would have been exposed to the teachings of their prophet Jesus of Nazareth. Because this Canaanite woman had sterling qualities that encompassed faith and persistence Jesus changed his mind.

We don't think of Jesus being subject to changing his mind. But changing one's mind, attitude, or activities, is not a sign of weakness. To change an attitude is not an easy. We seem to have an inbuilt resistance to change. To realise what you once thought true is not the truth, and change your attitude is a noble thing, indeed.

Can you squarely face up to the fact that some of your long held beliefs may be too small?

*Matthew 15:21-28; Mark 7:24-30*

# Martha

There are only two Gospel stories concerning Martha. In Luke's story Martha is serving the needs of family and guest and she wants her sister to help. As head of the household she should have been able to insist. Could it be that her younger sister was 'owned' by another?

Luke names more women than the other Gospel writers but he likes his women passive. In John's story we see a different Martha, though still a person of action, she goes out of the house and involves herself in pleading for her brother. Like Peter, she understands and confesses the nature of the Christ.

Martha is defined as a woman of leadership. Scholarship has never been able to agree as to exactly which Mary her sister is. Some have inferred she was a prostitute. This has been firmly discounted, but it is possible that Mary of Bethany is one and the same as Mary Magdalene. 'Magdalene' may not mean from Magdala but Magna meaning great, the Great Mary as distinguished from the Virgin Mary. Which may explain the surprising absence of this Mary at the cross and tomb. Tradition supports this stance.

There is compelling evidence to give substance to the tradition that the siblings from Bethany were expelled from Palestine with other Christians, condemned to float in a rudderless boat and arrived in the south of France. The three kinsfolk immediately began missionary activity in Marseilles. Lazarus is already a bishop and depicted in bishop's clothing. The first cycle of stories principally cluster round Mary Magdalene but an independent Martha tradition followed. Churches were named after her and surviving Christian art shows Martha performing a diverse range of activities. A famous painting on the altar at Tiefenbronn shows Martha comforting her brother on the voyage, cradling him on her lap. Other works show Martha as guardian to the Madonna and consecrating brother to a healing order named after her and many show Martha in the presence of a dragon.

The story goes like this:

In the countryside between Arles and Avignon there lived a terrible dragon monster who was described as half animal and half fish, fatter than an ox and longer than a horse, whose teeth were like pointed horns. The dragon was named Taracus. He particularly enjoyed submerging himself in the Rhone, sinking ships and killing any who tried to cross. The townspeople appealed to St Martha to save them from the dragon. Martha set out to find him. She was barefoot, wearing a long gown and carried nothing but a cross and a flask of holy water. He was not in the river, but she persevered and found him in a forest eating a man. She presented her cross and sprinkled holy water over the beast. He became as quiet as a lamb and she quickly took off her girdle and tied it round his neck as a lead thus taming the fearsome creature.

The theme of monsters threatening inhabitants is known in the mythology of most cultures. Usually the monster requires a sacrifice often a virgin. Eventually a hero appears and frees the latest victim, conquers the beast with force and finally slays the dragon. There are archetypal characteristics in the Martha legend by psychologically it is very different. Instead of a bound victim the dragon is bound, bound by a woman's magic girdle. The girdle has the power to tame ferociousness and conquer evil without resorting to violence. The female victim is replaced by a female heroine, against all the laws of mythology the woman is confronted with her like. Traditionally the woman is the embodiment of chaos, forbidding women are called 'old dragons' men are not, despite folk dragons being male creatures. This woman conquers that which is feared by women and thus is on a par with men.

St Martha's conquest of the dragon is strikingly different to St George's. George was aided by a stallion, armour, lance and sword. His story is of power and violence. The feminine version presents a vulnerable woman in long skirt and bare feet who overcomes without force. The patriarchal world takes pride in representing itself by conquest – a foot on the head of the dragon. The resurrection of Christ is likened to Christ trampling the serpents head. Martha symbolises another way of dealing with evil, not its annihilation but its redemption.

*Luke 10:38-42; John 11:1-44*

# Dispirited Women

Dinah • Tamar • Naomi • Michal

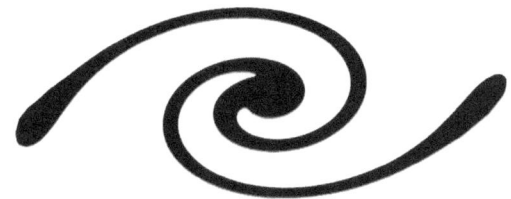

*Roar down our streets – winter gale blowing*
*sweep clean our dark places – hearts bare and renewed*

# Dínah • Tamar

The following piece is a different way of feeling into women of the Bible. It is an extract from a novel I co-authored with my son, Troy Sugrue. It is a thriller that juxtaposes the lives of women in the Bible with a group of women living Christchurch in 2009. The women are connected by Sarai who lectures on Women in Biblical Text at the university.

## *The League of Lilith* — An extract

### Chapter 12: Dinah and Tamar

"Sex," says Sarai. Without exception the students raise their eyes to hers, "Sex and Love. Both can happen without the other. Idealists would combine them, especially in marriage." She feels the full attention of the room. "I am sure each of you has an opinion on the matter. My interest, and I hope yours for the next 50 minutes, is the attitudes discernible in Hebrew Scriptures." She waits for the class to settle.

"Sexuality was no less important in ancient literature than it is in modern literature. Biblical sex is detailed in many forms ranging through love and hate, neglect, sensual erotica and sexual abuse. Some passages are gentle and others brutal. Most biblical marriages were arranged, and love was a low priority. In social, political, and economical terms the position of ancient women was vulnerable, but people were not in themselves very different from us. Some fell in love; others fell through lust.

"We will begin by looking at couples in Genesis and consider who may have been in love as viewed from our perspective." She moves to the whiteboard. "Let's name lovers. I want textual support for your contribution."

The class remains silent. "Come, start at the beginning. Ms Wakelin?"

The Goth replies lazily, "Adam and Eve I suppose."

"Anything to add, Ms Wong?"

"We don't know if Adam and Eve actually loved each other."

"Their options were rather limited," puts in Steve.

The class titters. Sarai says, "Possibly, Mr Paul, possibly."

"Remember Cain's wife," contributes Jake.

"Do you have an opinion on the quality of their relationships, Ms Finley?" Sarai turns her attention to the sweet-faced Rochelle.

"Adam and Eve are mythical characters, but the story implies they loved each other. Eve wanted to share with Adam and following their expulsion from Eden the narrator discusses the sexual desire that arises between husband and wife."

"A reasonable deduction," concedes Sarai. "Who features next in the biblical love stakes?"

"Sarah and Abraham," contributes Darlene.

Sarai raises a quizzical eyebrow. "Did Abraham treat Sarah well?"

"Well, he passed her off as his sister to save his own skin, but lovers can be cruel to each other. I think he loved her, because he wanted Sarah's child to be his heir not his firstborn son, and at his death the text says Abraham mourned and wept for her."

"Well done," Sarai nods, and Darlene blushes. "We are getting some credible suggestions, but I want facts. When is the word 'love' first mentioned in regard to a man and a woman?" Her eyes skim over the students and stop at Hana.

"Isaac and Rebekah?" she hazards.

"Reasons?" Hana shrugs.

"Ms Tombs?"

"When Isaac first saw Rebekah alight from the camel train the text says, he took her into his tent, and she became his wife and he loved her."

"Correct, and the next couple? Mr Jones, you may be able to help us here."

Jake grins and says, "Jacob and Rachel. My namesake was prepared to work a further seven years for the woman he loved."

Sarai adds the names to the whiteboard. "What about Jacob's children — have we scriptural proof that any of them loved or were loved?"

"Joseph," supplies the Goth reluctantly, cornered in Sarai's gaze.

"Certainly, loved by his father but in regard to his own love-life the Bible merely tells us Joseph married the Egyptian Asenath, a gift of the pharaoh, and she bore him two sons. The word love used in a sexual context appears in relation to only one other couple in the book of Genesis. Anyone?"

No suggestions are forthcoming. "The male in question is Shechem, the son of a prince. Genesis 34 words it thus: And his soul was drawn to Dinah the daughter of Jacob and he loved the maiden and spoke tenderly of her. The words convey strong emotion and would be charming if the previous verse had not conveyed something else — he saw her, he seized her and lay with her and humbled her. Are rape and love compatible? A rhetorical question, keep it in mind. Genesis informs us that Shechem did love the woman he raped and was prepared to go to great lengths to marry her. However, Dinah's full brothers were out for revenge, which they took by killing all the males of that town and plundering their property. Dinah is the pivotal character in the chapter but how she feels is never revealed. She has no voice and is given no dialogue. The Hebrew word for rape is from a root meaning to be bowed down, to be afflicted. Dinah is described as having been made unclean. It is implied that what she suffered was less than the offending that happened against her family — such was male understanding of rape.

We didn't touch on this incident in our initial look at Genesis as I want you to compare the Dinah scenario to a rape of Tamar in the Second Book of Samuel. Once again, the woman is described as beautiful and a virgin. She is another wealthy woman, this time a daughter of King David. She was also loved by a prince, a prince that happened to be her half-brother. She was tricked into performing an act of kindness for her brother Amnon, who claimed to be ill. He asked that she bake him some cakes and do it in his presence. Our English translations do not make it clear but in Hebrew Amnon requests that the cakes be heart shaped. Amnon watches but doesn't eat. He asks that the others present leave the room, then he grabs her.

The shocked Princess Tamar is given words: 'No, my brother, do not force me.' Her words are in vain and Amnon gets what he wants. His feelings are reported in full, chapter 13 verse 15: Then Amnon was seized with a very great loathing of her; indeed, his loathing was even greater than the lust he had felt for her. Amnon said to her, 'Get out!'

Amnon's response is not unusual. There is an abundance of current evidence to support the theory that many who dominate others are fighting what they perceive to be a weakness in themselves. Their victim's defeat reminds them of their own weakness and causes them to hate the victim. Does Tamar hate Amnon? We aren't informed but we are given Tamar's words: 'No, my brother for this wrong in sending me away is greater than the other you did to me.' Why? How could she possibly want to stay with her abuser? Ms Wong, do you have any light to shed?"

"She has lost her virginity and will not be acceptable to another as a bride."

"But what about the incest thing?" interjects Jake. "Weren't there rules? I thought the 'Law' was a big Hebrew thing."

"Royalty is not necessarily limited by the laws that govern commoners and this was certainly so in David's court. Tamar's pleadings can be read as suggesting 'you only need ask my father's hand,' but Amnon knows the reality: a beautiful daughter is a great asset to a king with alliances to form. All we know is Tamar rent her garments and cried bitterly. The last we hear of her is she remained a desolate woman in the house of her full brother Absalom. Amnon is not punished by his father. Is it because Amnon is David's eldest son, and heir to the throne? Absalom happens to be David's third son but the second son, Abigail's boy, is given no story so it is likely he died young. Two years later Absalom wreaks his revenge by arranging for the now unsuspecting Amnon to be killed at a sheep-shearing feast. This 'righteous revenge' action also advances Absalom in the line of succession. Once again, a woman is abused and male relatives take action supposedly on her behalf, when blood-lust and personal ambition is the heart of the issue.

The rapes of Dinah and Tamar have elements in common. The male scribes would have us believe that both perpetrators were motivated by love. After the abuse one rapist feels desire for his victim, the other hate. Both males die and both women are ruined. If these stories tell us anything it is that ancient man tended to confuse love and lust and ancient woman had to put security before love.

Confusing lust and love is not confined to the ancients. Modern women have far more choices but can feel just as powerless."

*Dinah: Genesis 34*

*Tamar: 2 Samuel 13*

# Naomi

They call me Naomi, it means sweet but when the famine came and my husband insisted we move to Moab, my nature soured. I knew such a place could not be sweet for Jews. How could Elimelech do this to us his when his name means 'my God is King.' But there was food in Moab and our sickly boys grew to men and married but I could not be happy in this land. How could I feel comfortable surrounded by Moabites, descendants of Moab, a man conceived through incest? These people were not my people and their God was not my God. The women our sons married carried the lineage of Lot and his elder daughter. How could I, a good Jewess, accept such women as my daughters?

But, I have to admit they were good girls, strong in themselves and willing workers. They tried their best to please me. Their heritage was not their fault but to me it just felt wrong. Their country was tainted with sexual impropriety. Ruth means pleasant, and indeed she was, too pleasant, in my opinion. Orphah was the practical one.

I was not surprised when my husband died. He had brought us to this sinful land. I came because I had no option ... and because I loved him. I wept for Elimelech when he was gone. My sons and their wives were kind, but I could not shake off the foreboding that worse was to come. And it did. Our offspring lived up to their names, Mahlon 'sickly' and Chilion 'early death.' Both died without out heirs. I was utterly bereft. My tears were bitter. I could no longer abide the sweet name Naomi. I was 'Mara' the bitter one.

The girls did their best to comfort me. I knew that I should be comforting them, but it was beyond me. They were young, they would find other husbands. To survive they must find other husbands. I made up my mind. I would return to the land of my birth, the land of my God and my forebears where I had relations and friends, the place where I belonged and where my husband owned property. The girls must return to their mothers and live the lives they were meant to live.

When I explained what I was doing they insisted on coming with me. They meant well but it was not what I wanted. Orphah understood, she kissed me tenderly and returned to her mother's house. But Ruth would not kiss me goodbye, she clung to me. I told her to follow her sister and return to her kin and her gods, but she would not. Instead of obeying me she stood and addressed me with a speech of undying love. The words were beautiful, and it should have been a beautiful moment ... but my heart was full of bitterness. Why did this young woman speak to me in this manner? Her intensity filled me with dismay. She had absorbed messages I had not intended. She used the language of covenant. Ruth believed she could be a Jewess! This Moabitess was turning her back on her own culture and was claiming mine, it was not only my culture she wanted, she wanted my love, more love than a mother-in-law can give.

I looked at her sadly, picked up my bundle of possessions and walked on. She followed me. No doubt she saw herself as a caring companion and my protector. But I did not want companionship on this journey. My name was Mara. I had no wish to talk nor did I care what might befall me. My Lord had turned against me. I had lost my husband and my sons. If I did make it back to Bethlehem ... Bethlehem, it translates to 'house of bread,' what wretched irony. I had left the house of bread for foreign food and now I was returning with a foreigner who would need feeding. My kinsfolk may accept me back but how would they feel about me bringing a Moabitess into their midst? We arrived at the beginning of the barley harvest.

Ruth asked if she may go and glean. It pleased me. We needed food. But was it safe for her to go out alone? Perhaps I should warn her of the young men who hovered around the gleaners, but I reasoned she was an intelligent girl quite able to take care of herself ... and there was a thought I did not want to admit to myself... in a dark recess of my bitter mind lurked a feeling that had she been molested I may be rid of her for good.

However, as luck may have it, or was it my God blessing my return, Ruth began her reaping in the field belonging to Boaz, who happened to be a wealthy young relative of my husband. There is no denying that Ruth was not only a tireless worker she was very pleasant on the eye. Boaz noticed the foreigner and her attributes. On learning to whom she belonged he offered her protection, and more, Boaz invited Ruth to eat with him, virtually welcoming her into the family. I learned all this when she returned with far more barley than expected. I could now accept a Moabite living with me; my foreign daughter-in-law had been accepted by the family of Elimelech.

It was a surprising turn of events. I dredged memories for details of Boaz. His name meant 'strength' or 'man of valour.' Then it came to me, his parents had done exceptionally well for themselves, but their union was not free from scandal. Salmon, the father of Boaz, had married Rahab! Boaz was the son of a Canaanite prostitute. My dark thoughts began to lighten. A clear path of action took shape.

The time of harvest came, carrying its eternal symbolic cycle of plenitude and fertility. I explained with care how its completion was celebrated and what my daughter should do. Ever willing to follow my instructions Ruth did as I advised. When she appeared before me bathed, perfumed and in her best clothes, even my senses were stirred, how much more would a man feel when merry wine.

The plan worked to perfection. A night of furtive passion unfurled on the threshing room floor. There was a slight hitch when a closer relative realised he was entitled to first option on Elimelech's field, but the man was quick to relinquish his claim on discovering a Moabitess came with the land.

But now, I am a grandmother! My friends are delighted for me. They say the child should be called Obed, meaning 'sought after.' I took the babe in my arms, smelt that tantalising infant smell, felt his soft, warm innocence as he snuggled against my breast, and discovered a child had been born to me. As joy seeped through these old bones. I understood a mighty truth, pedigree is not important, all children, whatever their heritage, culture, race, or religion, are gifts from God.


**Foot note:**

The child of Rahab and Salmon was Boaz; the child of Ruth and Boaz was Obed; the child of Obed was Jesse, the father of King David (the greatest king in Hebrew history was not of pure blood); and twice seven generations later the son of Mary and Joseph, Jesus (the greatest King in Jewish history was not of pure Jewish blood) nor was his lineage free from untraditional unions.

*See the genealogy detailed in Matthew 1:1-17*

### *Naomi and Ruth*

Naomi experienced famine and loss,
Ruth knew loss and unemployment.
One woman was old and bitter,
The other young and sad;
but each had courage
and journeyed in faith.
In the context of Harvest
they experienced blessing.

# Michal

The King is failing. The mighty David shivers in his bed. I watch from a window. The palace has many windows, ornate outer windows and secret inner windows. I see much and say little. I watch this husband but do not go to him. The King's advisors think a nubile beauty may rekindle his dying flame. How little they know!

The harem schemes, each minor wife sees herself as Queen Mother. Haggith's son has laid claim to the kingdom. He has no right. The insolent pup won't last. He is a coward at heart like his mother.

Bathsheba has more guts, even now she approaches. She turns her eyes from Abishag's curves but has no power to turn the tart away. Bathsheba may scheme for her royal child, but the woman remains a commoner. She grovels before David and calls him, "My King, my Lord."

"Little Princess" was his name for me. He did the bowing. Eighth son of Jesse; mere minion in my father's court; royal harpist; calming medication for the King; a shepherd-boy with the voice of an angel and the looks of a god... who couldn't walk in armour! Merab watched with haughty disdain. I stuffed a handkerchief in my mouth to control my giggles as the rural youth staggered in Father's armour. The tallest man in Israel lent his armour to a kid who fancied himself as a giant killer. My mad Dad! A general couldn't fill King Saul's armour.

My warrior father slowly going mad ... terrible to watch – the crazy mood swings, the mind that wasn't his. Physical illness is pitied, madness is scorned. There are many ways for the mighty to fall.

I loved my kingly father, so tall, so strong and so much man. As youngest, I was favoured, spoilt, his infant princess, his royal maid. Father-daughter love can be very special, but it cannot compare to man-woman love. Sensual love haunted my maiden self, tore at my flesh and addled my senses. Oh, foolish and innocent child that I was, I craved for the harpist. Long days spent listening for the sound of his voice and nights dreaming of his firm limbs entwined with mine.

Half the women of Israel were in love with him. For felling the Philistine, Merab was his prize. A country bumpkin betrothed to the king's eldest daughter! The lad was embarrassed. Merab was appalled. David was in awe of her. He smiled ruefully at me behind her back and went hunting with Jonathan whenever he could.

Merab had been groomed to marry well. She had a high born suitor. It was all so stupid, Merab wanting Adriel and me in love with the muso kid. We were friends, Merab and I. We bided our time. When father was in rational mood, we plied him with wine and asked our favours. He granted them. "So, maid Michal you love young David." Then the cunning crept into his eyes. I feared this madness, but it was too late. "If David wants you there must be a dowry."

When I heard the price, I knew Father was irretrievably insane, obsessed with violence and racked with jealousy. His illness knew no reason. The slaughter of a hundred men meant nothing. It was a scheme to kill a perceived threat to the throne. My beloved was hero material. He doubled the disgusting dowry and claimed me. My happiness defied description. My beloved was mine and I was his, but the banner over us was not love.

He confided his special destiny. My father's instinct had been right. I felt betrayed but how could I not love my hero husband. It seemed he was in no hurry to become king. He treated Jonathan more like his brother than mine. David had charm and easy confidence. Under my tutelage he quickly learnt our ways. His popularity knew no bounds. We had our own house and servants and Yahweh was our God. A god who cannot be seen is a difficult concept. My serving girl needed a visual aid. I let her have a teraphim, and just as well, or so I thought at the time, but Yahweh is a jealous God.

I could not be loyal to two kings. I made my choice. News of Saul's mania came via the servants. I drew the rope from its hiding place and secured it to a beam near the window. My maid placed the image in our bed as I helped David over the sill. With his breath hot on my lips I rehearsed lies and topped the teraphim with goat's hair. God grant I see him soon, I prayed. The capricious Yahweh granted my wish.

I saw my husband returning in the shelter of dusk. I called for a meal, made ready my hair and perfumed my couch. He came not. Then I glimpsed another man lurking in the shadows. I could not be mistaken. The figure was even more familiar than my husband. It was my brother, my beautiful brother Jonathan – Jonathan who made friends with armour bearers. A king's son takes his private pleasures as he likes. Many men disliked Jonathan but not all. I had seen lust light the eyes of his personal armour bearer and heard the youth say, "We are of one mind," I knew he meant, of one body.

From the widow of our bedchamber I watched and knew what I had hid from knowing. David, once amour bearer to my father, was fair game for Jonathan. This was no game. The embrace was not youthful horseplay. David was one of his ilk. This was a relationship, that other union that passes the love of women. David had used me to be near his heart's desire. Another woman I could understand, fight. But a man, my full brother – too much to bear!

Thank God David stayed away. I didn't want him. I would never want any man again. I sought out Merab for companionship. We were even closer in womanhood than childhood. I watched her beauty fade as she bore child after child. My regal sister lived oppressed by pregnancy and clamouring infants – four sons in as many years. Her vitality ebbed. Her womb dragged.

Adriel was a good man. He denied himself when he saw how wretched she was becoming. But she loved him, wanted him, and wanted a daughter. It was the fifth son that killed her. Adriel was beside himself with grief.

David had deserted me. I was legally free. I asked my father to give me to Adriel so I could raise his grandchildren. He agreed. Adriel was an Aramaic name. I chose to use the Hebrew form, Patiel. Alas Patiel's grief affected his mind. His illness was not like my father's. Patiel was never far from tears. He missed Merab too much to take me, not that he didn't love me, in his own pathetic way, but David had ruined love for me.

News of David's conquests filtered into Patiel's house. Long have I known the value of servant's ears and tongues. I learned of my replacement, Ahinoam of Jezerel and heard the saga of crafty Abigail. What David wanted David got. Bathsheba was a passing fancy that David killed for. Killing came easy to David: beasts, giants, husbands, sons, woman-love – not that he was without feeling. The bastard! Feeling was another of his accomplishments. Psalms and sackcloth. Drama and tears. When he wept, he wept! When he repented, he repented! When he partied, he partied! Whatever he did he did to excess. And David could do anything.

Anything, except form real relationships with women. Concubines galore. Serial wives, six of them, each with a single son. Daughters he couldn't relate to. Women made him nervous. When told of Tamar's rape by her half-brother he couldn't bring himself to punish his precious firstborn son. David's compassion found outlets in male eulogies. Women and land were for the taking. Rape and politics were his forte.

His God seemed to approve. Israel prospered under his hand as a united kingdom. I was called back into play as a political pawn. I didn't care the boys were old enough. They didn't need me. I felt some sympathy for Paltiel – he had been kind in his sad way. Part of me hankered to see David again, David in the flesh.

I saw more than I wanted. Didn't everyone! Dancing drunk, cavorting semi-naked in the street! I watched from the palace window. Revulsion was all I could feel for this man. Religious fervour was his excuse. The things people do in the name of religion! If this is what pleased his God, Yahweh could have him. David, who had sons beyond number, wanted a royal heir. The jumped-up farm hand was not getting one from the royal house of Saul. Clothed in his right mind David was more despicable than my father when ill.

Of course, the keeper of the records was not given the truth. It is unthinkable that a woman could refuse her husband let alone her king. How foolish are the thoughts of men – women crave sex, all women want sons. Refuse him I did. He was too humiliated to force me, but he got his revenge. Killed Merab's babies, my sons – spared Jonathan's cripple, and they say my father was insane!

I am Queen. The records cannot deny it so say nothing. My murder is literary. My life is silenced in the records but not in the court. The lesser wives scramble for final favours. Not one of them loved him as I loved. And not one of them hate him as I do. They think he loved them, and they are so wrong. I was his first. He was a virgin and I his virgin bride. He loved me as much as David can love any woman. I watch him suffer. He dares not dismiss Abishag. And, he can't keep his eyes off the untouchable butt of the luscious youth, ordered by me to calm the King with music.

• • •

This story is viewed through the eyes of King David's first wife, Michal, younger daughter of King Saul. All incidents contributing to the story can be found in the Bible in the First and Second Books of Samuel and Kings...

## References for Michal's story

| | |
|---|---|
| 1 Samuel 9:1-2 | Background and description of Saul |
| 1 Samuel 14:49-51 | King Saul's family |
| 1 Samuel 14:1-5 | Jonathan and his devoted armour bearer |
| 1 Samuel 17 | David kills Goliath |
| 1 Samuel 18:1-3 | Jonathan's soul in unison with David's soul |
| 1 Samuel 18:17 | Merab promised to David |
| 1 Samuel 18:19 | Merab given to Adriel |
| 1 Samuel 18:20 | Michal falls in love with David |
| 1 Samuel 18:21-31 | David wins Michal – dowry and marriage |
| 1 Samuel 19:1-10 | David at court with Saul and Jonathan |
| 2 Samuel 1 | David grieves over death of Saul and Jonathan |
| 2 Samuel 4:1-4 | Jonathan's son, Mephibosheth crippled |
| 2 Samuel 13 | Rape of Tamar |
| 2 Samuel 21:7-9 | David spares Mephibosheth, kills Merab's / Michal's sons |
| 1 Kings 1:1-4 | Abishag warms David in his old age. |

# Spirit Filled Women

**Hagar • Leah • Jephthah's Daughter • The Little Hebrew Maid • Elizabeth • Anna • A Woman at the Synagogue • A Woman of the Streets • Joanna • Lydia**

*Uplift and free us, help us to soar*
*May your energy power us, turn all hearts to you.*

# Hagar

From Slave Woman to Mother of a Nation

(A reflective dialogue suitable for presenting as a sermon)

**Hagar:**  My name is Hagar. It means flight. I was born on the banks of the Nile, born a slave in the house of the Pharaoh. When still a child I was given to Abram, a wealthy man with large flocks who had come to Egypt because of the famine in his land. Abram gifted me to his wife Sarai. The lady Sarai was born on the banks of the Euphrates. We have both travelled far from our homeland and kindred. I was very sad at being taken away from all I knew but the lady Sarai was kind. After a time, I found it exciting moving with this large household to unknown places. My master Abram believes his god will lead him to a promised land and make him father of a great nation. However, now there is bitterness abroad. Their god has let them down. We have been travelling for years and Sarai has no children. She was a great beauty in her day but now she is past her prime.

**Narrator:**  In ancient Hebrew understanding of conception and pregnancy the woman contributed nothing to the process. She was merely the ground for the man's seed. The seed was always considered fertile, but the receiving ground could be rich or barren.

To this point in the story Genesis records three visions of God promising Abram children. The couple's despair is understandable. While Abram anguishes Sarai acts. In matters concerning children women had considerable power. The maid, Hagar was hers to use as she pleased. The text tells of Sarai imploring Abram to take her slave so she, Sarai, may obtain children through her. Abram acquiesces without a word.

**Hagar:** A slave does as she is bid. I had to lie with my master. I was a virgin and it was no small matter to me. If I conceived my child would be Sarai's child. Surrogate motherhood is common, and distressing.

**Narrator:** The angry Sarai poured out her vengeance on Abram. He refused to accept any blame. 'Your slave girl is in your power, do to her as you please,' was his reply. Sarai dealt harshly with Hagar. The words pre-shadow the plight of the Hebrew slaves in Egypt, but Hagar was not liberated, she fled. Her Exodus did not bring freedom.

**Hagar:** Why should I accept such treatment from this woman! It wasn't my fault that I was pregnant. I didn't ask to be the sex slave of an old man. She didn't dare beat me because of the child but she berated me day and night. Abram did nothing to help me. I thought of a way to get back at her. If I disappeared there would be no child. That would fix the pair of them!

It was foolish really leaving the safety of the camp. My only plan was to try and get to Egypt. The wilderness is full of dangers, but luck was with me. After travelling a goodly distance, I found a spring. While I was resting an amazing thing happened. A stranger appeared and asked me from whence I came and where I was going. I didn't even feel afraid. I explained I was running away from my mistress.

The stranger told me I should return and submit. He spoke with authority and consideration, a mix so strange it occurred to me the stranger was no ordinary man. He told me that I would be blessed with a son and his name would be Ishmael and he would be the father of a great nation.

The stranger had to be and angel of the Lord. There was more, my child would grow to be a wild ass of a man living at odds with all his kin. Only a god could know such things. The angel was God himself. It burst on me as a revelation and I said, 'You are El-roi – the God who sees.'

I had seen God and lived! I named the place Beer-lahai-roi, that is well of the living one who sees me. I returned to my destiny and when my son was born, I told Abram to name him Ishmael which means God hears.

**Narrator:**  Hagar was the first woman to speak with God. God sought her by a well. The run-away slave behaved like a Patriarch. She named the place where she had met God and she named her son. That Abram allowed this is quite amazing, but even more amazing, Hagar named God. She is the only person in scripture to be so bold. Other women were promised sons but only Hagar was promised a nation. The reference to 'a wild ass of a man' was a compliment in a land where donkeys were highly prized.

The story does not end as a fresh reader may predict. There are yet more twists and turns. Sarai does not take Hagar's child as her own and the nation promised is not the nation promised to Abram. God again comes to Abram, reiterates former promises and assures him that the promise of an heir concerns his wife Sarai. To seal the covenant God gives them new names, Abraham father of many, and Sarah princess. This time they actually laughed at the news, but God being God had the last laugh. There was a child and God insisted they name him Isaac, 'he laughs.' Hagar's story continues in two versions. One tradition puts her son as an infant when Sarah delivers Isaac. The other tradition gives the boy's age as 13 years. Ancient stories were adapted to suit the times. Our challenge is to adapt them for our times.

**Hagar:**  It really was amazing old Sarah did have a son. When Abraham told her, yet again, she would be a mother, she laughed with derision. But the scorn turned to joy when a healthy son arrived. Abraham's God is very powerful. Sarah didn't bother me and life was calm until she one day noticed my lad playing with the toddling Isaac. It struck home to her that they were half-brothers. She went to Abraham and told him to cast me out. She didn't want any foreigner's son inheriting. The greedy 'Princess' wanted her child to get it all. I was banished. Abraham was quite upset. Not that he gave a thought to my plight. His thoughts were only for his son. Ishmael was three years old and pure delight.

**Narrator:**  God reminded Abraham that two people were about to suffer the boy and his slave woman. God comforted Abraham by assuring him that his first-born would also be the father of a nation. Abraham still didn't take his responsibilities on board.

**Hagar:** I awoke early and readied myself and my son for the journey. But where were the donkey and the men to guarantee us safe passage? All Abraham had for me was some bread and a skin of water. He kissed Ishmael and placed him and the meagre provisions in a sling on my shoulder. I wandered with my child in the wilderness until all the food and water was finished.

So much for God's promises, my son was going to die! The boy was dehydrated, lips cracked, and tongue swollen. I found a bush and laid him in its scant shade. 'Mummy, Mummy, he whimpered, drink, drink...' It was more than I could endure. There was nothing I could do. I couldn't bear to watch him die. I moved a little way off and gave way to my grief.

**Narrator:** God heard the voice of the child, so the scripture tells us. God must have also heard Hagar, because it was she who is spoken to. Her new status as a free woman is acknowledged for this time she is not addressed as 'Hagar, slave-girl of Sarai.'

**Hagar:** A voice penetrated my sobbing. 'What troubles you Hagar? Do not be afraid God has heard your child. Come lift him and hold him fast.' I ran to my son and hugged him. Then my eyes were opened, and I saw a well. From that moment I knew that God would protect us. We lived in the wilderness of Paran. My boy grew strong and became exceptional with the bow. When he was grown, I returned to the Pharaoh's household. My former master's son was impressed with my stories and with my son. I organised a royal bride for Ishmael. They gave me twelve grandsons, and each was a prince.

**Narrator:** The latter part of Hagar's story pre-shadows the Exile and Deliverance. The twelve princes link with the twelve sons of Jacob, and the land of Egypt grounds the plot. Ishmael established the Arab nation. Muslims and Jews claim relationship through their common father, Abraham. The bible records Isaac and Ishmael burying Abraham together. Any rift can be healed, be it between family members or nations. Hagar's story reads like a novel, and much of it is told from the woman's perspective. Imagine the women of ancient times spinning, weaving, gathered in tents or round campfires, honing these stories for their children.

The content of Hagar's story is both novella and parable. The woman's name, Flight, describes her life but Hagar was able to rise above her station. The women spoke of a God who aligns with the marginalized and the oppressed. They could tell their children; God hears the cries of the distressed. God made a Covenant with Abraham, the rich and powerful Patriarch but God also made a Covenant with an abused woman.

Hagar heeded God and took responsibility for herself. In so doing Hagar was transformed from victim to victor.

*Main stories: Genesis16:1-15; 21:1-20*
*Other related readings: Genesis 12:10-20; 17:1-27; 18:1-15; 25:1-11*

## God Who Sees

God we come before you confident that you are God; you see and hear and speak:
God who sees ... **Help us to be women (people) who see.**

God we come before you confident that you are a God who hears:
God who hears ... **Help us to be women (people) who hear.**

God we come before you confident that you are a God, who speaks:
God who speaks ... **Help us to be women (people) who speak.**

Enable us to challenge outmoded ways of being, believing, and speaking:
God who challenges ... **Help us to be women (people) who accept challenge.**

Enable us to be honest in our search for faith and to find wisdom:
God who understands ... **Help us to be women (people) who understand.**

Enable us to be aware and use words that encourage those around us to seek life and truth in ways appropriate to present times:
**Help us to be women (people) who know how to serve our times by using our time well. Amen.**

# Leah

My sister has returned from the well breathless with news of stranger who rolled the stone from the well so she could water the flock. Her cheeks are flushed. The gentleman claims to be a distant kinsman. "Come and see she urges." My father runs after her shouting, "Surely you are my flesh and bone, my sister's son." He embraces the stranger and invites him to stay with us for a month. It is rather exciting a cousin arriving out of the blue, and a handsome one at that. I am a woman of marriageable age. Rachel is still a child. She is a pretty child and graceful in movement. Although I tend to be short sighted, I see her eyes light up whenever Jacob enters. He calls her his little ewe lamb. The way he looks at her is not how one should look at a child. My eyes may be a little weak, but my lashes are long and curling. Beautiful cow's eyes my father says. In herding he prefers sheep. Distance may blur and wrinkle my brow, but I do not lack insight.

My father strikes a deal with Jacob, for seven years labour he may marry Rachel. The month of Jacob's visit extends to seven years. Jacob boasts it is as if a few days because of his love for Rachel. In all this time my father has made no effort to find me a bridegroom. He has not looked among the men of Haran and no further marriage-seeking cousins have enriched the horizon. Our brothers have wives. Why are daughters so dependent on fathers? Why can we not choose our own destiny?

Rachel is beside herself with joy because my father's friends are gathering for the wedding feast. I note Laban has the look of a beguiler in his eye and wonder why. At night he confides his plan, he intends both of us to marry Jacob. He wants me to go to the bridal chamber, to speak not a word, and stay heavily veiled until it is too late.

Do I want Jacob? His desire is for my sister and his name means trickster. Do I want to be a pawn in my father's game? And what of my young sister, can our closeness survive this manipulation? But my survival depends on marriage and my father is determined.

All happened as my father wished. Jacob was furious but Laban calmed him with smooth assurance that it is the custom of this place to marry the elder first and he may have Rachel in a week, as long as he will work a further seven years. As for me I do the best I can. Loved or not I am head wife and I take my responsibilities seriously. Our household has many servants.

It seems, however, that my sister and I are both barren. Neither of us has become pregnant. Is it because my father tricked Jacob into marrying the two of us, or is it because Jacob carries sins from his past? He tricked his twin, Esau, out of his rightful inheritance. Are we to reflect the mirror image of his sibling rivalry, and become puppet characters in a male tale, where a man is punished through his women!

I know Jacob loves Rachel more than me but also know he does not dislike me. I believe the Lord has taken pity on me because at long last I am pregnant and Rachel remains empty.

I name our firstborn Reuben see, a son, because I know the Lord has seen my affliction and dealt kindly with me. He continues to deal kindly with me – Simeon, Levi, and Judah, arrived in swift succession. I am wearied with childbirth and losing my figure. The taunts of barren Rachel are worse than the taunts of virgin Rachel. She claims I named my sons to upset her. This is paranoia. The names hearing, adhesion and praise were not chosen with her in mind. Rachel is verging on hysteria. She begs Jacob to give her children. Jacob retorts he isn't God; he hasn't made her barren. She was so upset she asks him to have children by her own servant girl. Rachel names Billah's sons Dan and Naphtali. This got me thinking, why should I bear child after child? I have my own maid. If Jacob wants a tribe let him have his pleasure with her. Zilpah produces Gad and Asher. Alas, now Jacob has so many young wives he has forgotten me.

My offspring are growing into fine young men. They tend the fields. Reuben, my kind-hearted eldest, discovers a patch of mandrakes amongst his wheat. Everyone knows mandrakes have special powers. Reuben brings the mandrakes to me. Rachel asks that I give some to her. We talk and find strength in sisterhood. We decide that even though we can't control our bodies we can control our husband. We will decide which of us sleeps with Jacob. I am given two more sons and a daughter. Then Rachel is blessed with a son. I believe it is because we co-operated that Rachel was able to get pregnant. I am pleased for her even though it distresses me that Jacob favours her Joseph over all the others.

Jacob continues to prosper by trickery with Laban's flocks. He also sees that Laban does not think upon him as favourably as before. Discontent is rife. Our father makes it plain to us that he intends us no further inheritance. We feel he has sold us and that we are now as foreigners to him. Our husband and our father are both cheats. There is no escaping the trickery of men!

Jacob suddenly decides his God wants him to return to his own land. It's our belief he wants to parade his prosperity and we speak with one voice. We agree to his proposal. We might as well see something of the world beyond our father's fields. The plan is not to inform our father lest he cause trouble. We prepare in secret, packing personal possessions, sorting household goods, and storing food.

When I discover Rachel had stolen some of our father's gods I am greatly worried. I can understand her wanting to keep something precious from our own house, but this is foolish. I cannot dissuade her. Our mother was fertile, and these are fertility gods. I know her desperate hope for another son. The gods are in her camel's saddlebag when the caravan moves.

Naturally our father Laban is enraged. He pursues in hot anger. Trickery begets trickery. Rachel fools all the men. But she does not know Jacob has sworn death to the thief if discovered in his camp.

I see Laban in a new light. He is a parent, and like all parents is ambitious for his children. Not only ambitious he loves us. This passion is not only for his household gods, he regrets our leaving. He wants to ensure that Jacob will treat us well. The men make a covenant swearing honour and respect. When it is done our father kisses us and all his grandchildren and gives his blessing.

We continue our journey and are well received by Jacob's twin. It gladdens us all to be part of such a fervent reunion. Alas, other violence corrupts my own children and brings me heartbreak. And now my dear sister lies beneath a pillar in a no-place on the way to Bethlehem. Rachel died in childbirth. Had trickery not filtrated our family she would not have been cursed. I keep our guilty secret to myself. Jacob is as sad as I am. At the end Rachel called the child Benoni, son of my sorrow. But for the first time Jacob asserts his authority in naming. He decrees his twelfth son be named son of my right hand. All we can do is lavish our affection on baby Benjamin.

*Genesis 29:15-35*

# Jephthah's Daughter

## Jephthah

What have I done!
I wanted might,
And I got might.
This cursed bastard is a mighty warrior.

What have I done!
I wanted revenge,
And I got revenge.
My spiteful half-brothers and their
righteous friends begged my help,
And they got it, on my terms.

What have I done!
I wanted power,
And I got power.
I managed the negotiations.

What have I done!
I wanted to be seen as virtuous
And I bargained with the Lord
I made an impressive public vow.

What have I done!
I wanted fame
And I got fame;
I made the greatest sacrifice a father can make,
My only child
Oh, what have I done?

## Jephthah's Wife

That child was not only your child,
She was our child.
Our daughter that I gave birth to,
the daughter that only I loved.

Your obsession for might and revenge,
your greed for power, virtue, and fame
gave you nothing of worth.
Your selfishness took, stole, and robbed…
our child of her life, me of my darling girl,
and you, of the only thing you really wanted…
but you were too stupid to see it.

I gave myself to you,
Our daughter offered delight to you,
but you were too self-consumed to respond.
Now all you will ever feel is hate and disgust.

Your pretentious vow earned no virtue.
You saw our daughter as expendable.
Well, consider this, you vile fool.
The reason your half-brothers wanted
you to lead their battle was only
because they saw you as expendable.

Murderer, don't ape innocence to me,
our daughter honoured you as tradition
expects maidens to greet victors;
But you in your sordid wish to impress
blamed the victim for being where she was.
Your pathetic bid for sympathy
impressed only the gullible.

The name Jephthah will be noted and despised.
But, I know with gut certainty, that even if
our daughter's name is omitted from the records,
She will be remembered with respect and affection.

# Jephthah's Daughter

Do not cry for me, Mother dear,
Ours is a love that can never be lost.
Live well a life ripe with years
knowing that I live on in love.

Do not grieve with hate, Mother dear,
Hate is a horror beast that can hurt the hated
but always harms the hater more.
The groom who claimed you as his bride
was a damaged man
and despite your best efforts
you could not undo what had been done;
The abused child became a child abuser.

Do not be sad for me, Mother dear,
spare sorrow for him to whom you are wed.
Though brash in his attempt at being pious,
he is unable to feel into the realm of the Spirit.
No understanding would have been achieved
by reminding him of Abraham and Isaac;
even Abraham, who loved the Lord,
failed to grasp what the Lord required of him.

Do not despair for me, Mother dear,
God gave me strength and clarity of vision.
Did you not see that it was me who took control?
I passed judgment, on Jephthah's words and willingness
to bargain glory, for the life of any living soul.
My actions condemned all warped wishes.
God was with me.
Now I am with God;
able to understand more than before.
Men use words that assign women
roles of androcentric presumption.
But a time is coming when we
will not have to live by their rules
or pretend to be what we are not.
Meanwhile, do not let any man define
what you are, or who you are.

God helped me bargain enough time
to share spiritual insights with my friends.
We girls had a wonder-filled time together,
being young with laughter, song, and tears,
talking and listening, learning and loving,
running free, dancing and praying.

My friends made a pact to do it again,
not just next year, but every year.
And, not just with young women
but with all women who want to be
what our God wants us to be.

Yahweh is not a war God,
a jealous God, a judging God;
Yahweh is a Parent God,
ever loving and creating,
not only King of Heaven
but Queen of Heaven too.

Weep when you need to, Mother dear
but know I am with Hagar's God,
El-roi, the God who sees…
and hears and understands.

The heavenly odours
that best please
Our Mother-Father God
are the homely smells
of cooking food to share.

Next year, Mother dear, remember me
by gathering your friends, then
go adventuring with my friends
and the God that Hagar named.

Surrounded by female soul mates
we are free to be who we really are.
Go, show and share what being woman truly means…
and, bake heavenly cakes for Heaven's Queen.

*Judges 11; Genesis 16:13; Jeremiah 44:19*

# The Little Hebrew Maid

Among the many international ills is the terrible plight of the displaced people throughout our world. In our comfortable paradise it is easy to become complacent especially when we live in an area where we are unlikely to encounter many refugees. But whenever there is war, disaster, injustice and greed there are refugees. There have been displaced persons from the beginnings of civilization. Now technology has shrunk the world, people are more readily displaced and dispatched than ever before. Countries that have offered refuge in the past are finding they cannot cope. It is becoming near impossible to absorb the vast numbers of desperate displaced persons who have nowhere safe to call home. To have your personal world destroyed and be left without your country is unimaginable to us – but let's try…

Think yourself into the life little girl in a devout Hebrew home. You are happily playing one day when raiders appear, they kill your parents, burn your house and snatch you as a trophy of war. In a state of absolute terror, you are taken by the murderers, dragged away from everything you ever knew and placed as a slave in a heathen household.

Such a girl is mentioned in the Hebrew Scriptures, a very brief mention, but her role is pivotal in one of the greatest healing stories of the Bible. Here we meet a child victim who feels compassion for her captors. What an amazing thing! There is no doubt that trauma ruins lives, but trauma does not ruin all lives. Some victims are able to rise above their changed circumstances. Where does their inner resource come from? Many attribute it to faith in God, and we know, inner strength is easier to access if a person has known love. With victims healing is more likely to happen if the victim experiences understanding and kindness. We can presume that the Little Hebrew Maid, as she is known, came from a loving and Godly family, and despite the shocking events that led to her being a maid, she was treated decently by her wealthy mistress.

The facts we are told are about her master, Naaman. Naaman is a great man, Commander of the army of the king of Aram. He has many victories to his credit, but the mighty warrior Naaman falls victim to the dreaded disease leprosy – terribly distressing for him and his wife.

When I was a girl, I attended Girl Guide church parades in the three mainline protestant churches in my town. Most imposing was the Anglican with polished brass, stained glass and gowned choir. Perhaps the ambience helped the sermon stick. The vicar presented this story as a model for girls. We were impressed – **a girl hero in the Bible!** Details dull over the years but I'm pretty sure the vicar avoided the unpleasantness of the girl's abduction and concentrated on 'serving her master' like we girls should willingly serve those in authority over us. That is how tales were told in those days – Bible stories for children were always given a moral.

Many feminist years later I agree the Little Hebrew Maid was a hero but not for the reasons the vicar gave. She was able to rise above her personal trauma to live as a person of faith and compassion. She retained belief in her God and the God given abilities of her homeland prophet. She perceived the anguish of her captor as a person in need. She did what she could to help. She bravely shared her faith with her mistress. Of course, the child is not credited or even named. In a story of 27 verses she is allocated only 2 but without the Little Hebrew Maid there would have been no story to record. And the story is a great story – a tale of pomp and circumstance, pride and prejudice, appreciation and greed, but as this book is a herstory selection you will have to read it for yourself!

*2 Kings 5*

# Elizabeth

I had a special dinner waiting for Zechariah. I was so proud of him! As you know Anna, not many small-town priests get the honour of entering the Holy of Holies. I'm so glad you saw him go in. Didn't he look fine in his robes? If only you had been there when his duties were over! He arrived home in a terrible state. He tried to tell me what had happened, but he couldn't speak – not one word could he get out. I was really worried and thought he had contracted some terrible illness. But he looked healthy enough, in fact he looked…radiant is the word that comes to mind. Well, there he was flinging his arms around and trying to mime something. This is crazy, I said, and went and got the slate.

When I read what he had written I was staggered. But then, I thought, why shouldn't my husband receive a vision. He is a good man. And he is married to a good woman. I've never believed barrenness to be a punishment for wrongdoing. Many good women have been barren – Rachel, Hannah and Samson's mother. But when Zec gave my hand an impulsive squeeze reality kicked in. His knuckles are misshapen with arthritis. We are an elderly couple. Then I thought of Sarah and I clasped these worn hands in a little prayer of delight.

Zech was keen to go to bed right there and then but I wasn't having a good meal wasted. I'd put a lot of love into this dinner – his favourite food, special candles and all. Besides, Zech had walked a long way and he needed to keep his strength up.

I was pregnant within the month. I didn't dare believe it for months but deep down I knew. Well over forty and never felt fitter! Even so I was little embarrassed and kept myself well hidden. But we got a visitor. It was my cousin's girl, Mary, the one engaged to Joseph, the carpenter. She should have been at home preparing for the wedding. It was a shock seeing her. I hadn't told anyone. But she knew! She hugged me and called me blessed.

I know I can trust you Anna… the thing is the girl was pregnant. Don't breathe a word of this. It is a difficult situation… the child isn't Joseph's. Yet, when she told me she wasn't distressed. Turns out, she too had been blessed with a vision. The very moment Mary told me she was pregnant my child leapt in my womb. I'd felt little flutters before, but this was a real kick, a kick of joy. I knew it was a sign.

Mary stayed for three months. We crafted our own song of joy based on Hannah's. We did our exercises together and made baby clothes. She does exquisite work for one so young – you should see her swaddling cloths! It was a good thing Zech couldn't talk because he wouldn't have got a word in edgeways! Of course, I did feel sorry for him, especially after our son was born. He so wanted to bless him.

The child was perfect. The birth hadn't been too bad. The labour was strong but steady. The midwife said I was pushing well. Young Mary was a great help, sponging my brow, rubbing my back and clasping my hand. I was so tired but what a wonderful feeling holding my own baby, a son for Zechariah. He didn't need words to tell me he loved me.

The neighbours were all around with little gifts. They were astounded when I told them our boy would be called John. There are no Johns in your family they said. You must call him after your husband. They mean well, but really, who do they think they are!

Anyway, they pestered Zechariah asking him to nod agreement. Instead he reached for his slate and wrote the child's name is John. Why John they shrugged? "John," shouted Zechariah, "is the name God has chosen." Well, that knocked them for a six, really shut them up. Zech and I just hugged each other and didn't care what the neighbours thought. We had our son. We had each other and God had lifted his punishment. Life can be wonderful Anna.

*Luke 1*

# Anna

I am an old woman and I have seen many things. I was widowed when my son was but six years old. My daughters were one and four. But I managed. God took care of us. They grew to be fine people and have families of their own. I will be grateful all my days. It is my privilege to serve God with prayer and fasting. With humbleness I accepted the title prophetess, but I felt it had been awarded without due merit. I am just an ordinary woman with ordinary fears.

I fear for this land of ours so long occupied by Rome. There is much unrest, and many godless people. Yet recently I have seen signs of hope. I am starting to believe that a messiah will come and deliver Israel from her oppressor. I dare think that such a one has been born. I talked this over with my old friend Simeon. He listened carefully and agreed it could be. He told me that once he had dreamed he would not die until he had seen the messiah. I believe God's spirit is with Simeon. He is a good man, a devout man, and so good with words. But he's not as quick at picking up on signs and feelings as I am. So, we wait in hope and encourage each other.

I saw the child first. I recognized the mother, Mary, kinswoman to my good friend Elizabeth. I recalled the strange connection between the pair and suddenly I just knew! "That's the child," I breathed. Simeon paused only long enough to gaze from my eyes to the child's. Understanding flooded his soul as it had mine. He took the child and praised God with the eloquence of a psalmist.

Then it was my turn. I held the blessed infant and told the surprised parents that his was no ordinary child. This child had the potential to save Jerusalem and yea, the whole world. As I gazed at the peaceful bundle, I knew the way to salvation was not by the sword. I said to all who would listen, "A new order is coming. This child is the prince of peace."

*Luke 2:36-38*

# A Woman at the Synagogue

Imagine the Synagogue with its bustle of religious men performing their religious duties. This particular Sabbath a visiting preacher captures a large audience. Behind a grill, women, children and slaves gather to watch. One person, more outcast than the rest, slouches alone. Children stare and mothers pull them away. The outcast bears the stigma of sin – a curse that renders her a cripple. She exists with the burden of living bent over for eighteen years, denied easy glance to sky and faces. Her wretched and painful world is that of feet, dust and mud. She must have done something terrible to merit this. She survives by begging. Her only hope is to be as religious as possible.

Anticipation rises as the guest speaker mounts the rostrum. He gazes over the crowd. He is young and confident. His eyes light upon the misshapen shadow beyond the grill. "Woman," he calls, "Come here." The crowd is astounded, and shocked. Men do not speak to women in the Synagogue, and women do not enter the main portion. All this woman wants is to worship unnoticed, but she dares to obey.

Feel her hating the gaze of the public; imagine her pause in panic; notice the crowd move back; see the disgust on their faces; she does not twist to look but she feels the disdain. An unpleasant murmur ripples the crowd and over it comes the voice of Jesus saying, "Come unto me."

Mustering all the courage she can gather the woman limps forward, on and on, through the hostility right to the front. Jesus stoops and touches the untouchable one. The touch is warm, human, tender and strong. "Woman," he says, "You are freed from your infirmity." She straightens to his words and looks into the face of the Christ. The crowd is transfixed, and angry.

Not only has an unclean woman entered a sacred part of the synagogue, the healer is 'working' on the Sabbath. The young preacher dares answer his elders and betters with a ring of authority. He calls them hypocrites reminding them that they tend animals on the Sabbath.

Then Jesus refers to the deformed woman as a 'daughter of Abraham.' Abraham! The greatest of the Patriarchs, the founder of the Nation, the 'great one' prepared to follow God to the end of the world, the person of perfect faith with whom God made a holy Covenant. To be called a daughter of Abraham elevates her to undreamed of status.

Those present witnessed more than a mere healing. All are confronted with the fact that this non-person is their equal. She is their sister. Jesus further reminds the people it is not sin but Satan that bound their kinswoman. The people understand and are ashamed. And then, they are able to rejoice.

*Luke 13:10-17*

Loving God,
We acknowledge that regardless of health,
attitude, appearance or status,
we are people marred by imperfections.
Grant us the strength to manage our infirmities
with wise caring, good humour, and gratitude.
Help us use whatever we have to become
more insightful to the conditions of humans,
and more attentive to matters spiritual.
Save us from falling victim to self-centredness
– a malaise that preys on the fit and the unfit
that left unchecked is more soul destroying
and more binding than any physical aberration.
In the loving of others may we find perfection. Amen.

# A Woman of the Streets

I was there that day when he rode into to Jerusalem. It was the first day of the week. On the other side of the city citizens were gathering to welcome Pontius Pilate, the Roman governor of Idumea, Judea, and Samaria. He would enter at the head of a column of cavalry and horses, a display of military might and grandeur. I'd seen such processions before. The imperial procession would have been unaware of the peasant procession on the west side of Jerusalem. I wonder if either will be remembered in years to come?

When I heard that the teacher and his following were going to Jerusalem for the Passover, I decided I must get myself to Jerusalem, this year! I had a premonition that it was important. It was the same urgent feeling I felt when I heard him speak in the City of Nain. I had never heard anyone speak as Jesus did. He seemed to be speaking directly to me, assuring me that no matter what I had done he understood, and God would forgive me. I felt it was actually possible to turn my life around. Jesus was more than an ordinary man. Others were impressed by his healing touch. He was the toast of town after raising the widow's son.

When I heard that the Pharisee Simon had invited Jesus to dine at his house, I felt I had to let him know that I understood his message and do what I could. I had to thank him before he left town. I've had my share of rich clients. Now I had no desire to keep their gifts. I traded them all for an alabaster jar full of precious ointment. In my heart I felt this teacher was as important as a king. Of course, a woman like me couldn't say these things, and who would listen if I did? But no one seemed to understand how important Jesus was. Real kings were anointed by prophets. I was only a woman and a sinner at that. I wouldn't dare presume to touch the head of so great a person, but I could touch his feet. Washing the feet of guests is a servant role.

I was no stranger to Simon. He dared not turn me away when I walked in unannounced. His eyes narrowed but I faced them squarely. There were many guests and lots of servants milling round with dishes of food. I took my place at the feet of Jesus. His feet were dusty. All the guests had dusty feet. This was insulting. It was common courtesy to wash the feet of guests before a formal meal. How could Simon be so common and careless in his hospitality!

As I looked at the feet of Jesus a great sadness came over me. Something dreadful was going to happen to these strong feet, I just knew it. I began to cry, softly. The tears streamed and cleansed those dear feet. All I had to dry them with was my hair. I kissed his feet and soothed them with ointment.

Simon saw what I was doing, if looks could kill, I know where I would be. His lips moved as he muttered to himself. I could guess his thoughts, and I was not the only one. Immediately Jesus called for silence and told a story about a creditor who forgave two debtors. He asked Simon which debtor would love the creditor more, the one who owed the small debt or the one who owed the large debt? Simon had no idea what he was talking about, but I did.

Then Jesus reminded Simon that he had neglected some of the duties of a good host. I suspect Jesus would have mentioned these things had I not been there. I think he said what he did because he knew Simon was insulting me.

Since that day I have sought and found honest employment as a maid, but last week I took time out to go to Jerusalem. I understand life on the streets. I heard of a donkey borrowed by his followers and kept watch on the house. Now Jesus is riding through the streets. It is only a humble donkey he is riding but the crowd is going wild. They are tearing palms-leaves from the trees and waving them, shouting Hosanna. It is if they think he will save them from the Romans. It is a spontaneous expression of joy. Why do I feel so sad?

*Luke 7:36-50*

# Joanna

I don't know what happened. All I know is that when I went to the Tomb He wasn't there. It had all been so terrible, our beloved teacher betrayed and treated with such atrocious cruelty. It was too much for most of the men to bear. But we women stayed, it was all we could do, be there. As women we know pain and we know how it is to be helpless. I think it is harder for men. They so feel they must do something.

It was some comfort to know he had a decent tomb and linen burial cloths. I made it my business to thank Joseph of Arimathea. The others were overawed with him being a member of the council. Coming from the court of Herod I know how to address men of rank. He appreciated the acknowledgement. For myself I was pleased that my funds had lasted sufficiently to buy the spices and perfumes that should accompany a noble burial.

We women were wondering how we would move the stone but when we arrived the stone was rolled away. We were very worried and wondered if the body had been stolen, and why. We entered and the tomb was empty. It's hard to describe what happened, none of us can recall it accurately. It was unreal, a vision I suppose, light, angels, or perhaps men in dazzling garments. Whatever it was we were scared and flung ourselves to the ground, so didn't really get a good look, but one thing we can agree on was voices, we all heard the same message, "Why do you seek the living among the dead?" Some thought they heard more words but I'm not sure. I'm not even sure the voice came though sound, it was more something I felt. The light vanished and so did we. We ran all the way back to the disciples. They were not inclined to believe us. But Peter decided to check the grave and he saw for himself the folded linen.

Later Mary was sure she encountered Him in the garden. She told us she was crying so much she could hardly see. I wonder if she heard a voice much as I did. I don't know what happened and I don't know where He is. But He doesn't seem far away. He seems particularly near when I am alone in a garden. The new growth of the spring reminds me there is always hope, despite winter life goes on. All flowers wither and vanish then months later they reappear as beautiful as ever.

It is autumn now, and in this garden, exotic trees are turning red and gold. Leaves are covering the ground in soft drifts of colour. The colour won't last but for now it is stunning. The fallen leaves are the colours of wine and crusty bread. I drink it in and store the memory. I remember the things He taught us. His words nourish my soul. I know his work is continuing. The Apostles are spreading the word and groups of believers are quietly meeting in many, many places. Leaves are like His words they fall and nourish the earth. Soon they will fade and vanish, but their goodness is not wasted. Goodness is never wasted.

*Luke 8:3; 24:12*

## Garden Blessing

Circle this place by day and by night,
May cycling seasons bring delight.
In this small garden may you smile
and walk content with us awhile.
Keep us aware of things that harm,
and guide us to your healing balm. Amen.

# Lydía

Life has many twists and turns. When I think about it, I realise I have led a surprising life. Many women live their entire lives near their place of birth, following the life pattern of their mothers and grandmothers before them, not me!

I was born in Thyatira, in the district of Lydia. My birthplace was a significant trade centre sited on the crossroads of trade flowing between Constantinople and Palestine. Thyatira was noted for numerous trade guilds – bronze-smiths, wool workers, linen-workers, leather-workers, tanners and dyers. My husband was a dyer. His was a quality product, a red-purple dye, made from the root of the madder plant. The plant grows well in our area. I took a interest in his trade. I like the excitement of commerce and the bustle of the marketplace. I developed an eye for cloth and became a skilled trader. I developed quite a reputation and became known as 'the seller of purple.' Sometimes traders brought blue-purple cloth to our market. This product was made from the gland of a shellfish abundant on the Phoenician Coast. The dye was inferior to our purple. It occurred to me that we had a product that could find clients among wealthy Roman officials.

So, to cut a long story short, we moved, travelling across the Aegean Sea to Philippi. My hunch was right. We established a thriving business selling purple that originated from our hometown some 65 miles to the north-west. Because we came from Lydia we were known as 'the Lydians.' We built a fine house and had many servants. Life was good until my husband succumbed to an illness and died. I was able to continue the business. I had the support of women friends. Some of my friends were Jews. There was no Synagogue in Philippi, so the Jewish women used to gather at the river to pray. I was impressed by their devotion and keen to learn more of their God. They called me Lydia and likened me to Ruth the Moabitess. She was a foreigner who did well for herself and has become part of their heritage. Not many women are remembered in history. It would be rather nice to have one's story told through the ages.

Surprisingly, one Sabbath some visiting men joined our little company of women. They were teachers with a new message. They told of a man named

Jesus whom they believed to be the Son of God. They called this Jesus, the Christ. They said he proclaimed a new order a new way to live, a way of love that respected all people. The God of Jesus was a loving God who cared for everyone. I listened eagerly this was indeed good news. In fact, I was so impressed I invited the travellers to stay at my house. And now I am convinced this was the best thing I have ever done!

Paul was a wonderful teacher. I became a convert to this new Christian religion. I asked to be baptised with my entire household. It was a time of great rejoicing. But more drama was to come. One day while out preaching Paul healed a demon-possessed slave girl. Her masters had been using her illness as a public spectacle for gain. When cured the girl no longer made strange utterances. Deprived of their livelihood her masters had Paul and Silas flogged and put in prison. The Romans can be very cruel. I was in a dilemma I wanted to help my guests but what could I do against Roman authorities! That night there was an earthquake. I wondered if God was showing anger at this injustice. Late next day Paul and Silas returned to me. I was amazed to see them. They looked remarkably well. Their wounds had been dressed! They told us this amazing story. The earthquake had loosed their chains, but they had not fled. Instead they had stopped the jailer from harming himself. If prisoners escape no mercy is shown the jailer, and he was about to take his own life, but Paul convinced him no one had escaped. The jailer was so grateful he fed them and dressed their wounds and spoke on their behalf. Paul and Silas were told they could go but they didn't. Can you believe this?

I found it difficult, but it turns out Paul was actually a Roman citizen and he demanded to be treated like one. He would not go until he had received an official apology from the authorities. And what is more, he got it!

Paul and Silas left within a few days, but my life was changed forever. Now I treat the lesser members of my household quite differently. Even slaves and jailers are children of God. I have opened my home to people in need. My house has become a centre for any intent on living the Christian life. I host the church of Philippi. Who would have thought that an impulsive act of hospitality could make such a difference! My house is truly blessed.

*Acts 16:11-40*

# Other Notable People

Oded • Argula von Grumbach • Susanna Wesley
• Ann Turner • Lenna Button

*Breath of the Spirit come blow among us
fill and inspire us, with life-giving joy.*

# Oded

Oded is not a woman but is included because of what he did to save a great number of women and children from a very bleak future. His story needs to be told and shared.

Oded is a minor prophet buried away in Scriptures that are seldom read, yet the one incident concerning him is recorded is amazing. Oded lived during the period when the Northern and Southern Kingdoms of Israel and Judah were squabbling among themselves. It is recorded that King Ahaz of the Southern Kingdom did not walk in the ways of his ancestor David and did great evil to the Jewish faith. According to the world-view of the chronicler, God let Ahaz suffer military defeats. The victorious army of Israel led by the Northern King Aram took captive 200,000 women and children, and along with much booty, dragged them off to their Northern capital, Samaria.

Imagine the scene…

The soldiers weary from marching but gloating in victory dragging and prodding a massive number of exhausted captives. They have walked for days and have parched throats and aching limbs. Many stumble along in the unrelenting heat without shoes or adequate clothing, including women carrying infants they can't feed and traumatised children. The city populace is gathered to cheer the soldiers and jeer at the prisoners.

But before the crowd could voice what was expected of them the prophet Oded went through the city gates and stopped the procession. The prophet berated the soldiers saying their actions had gone too far and God was angry with their behaviour. Oded refused to accept the captives, declaring they would not pass into the city as prisoners.

Oded began as one solitary voice of conscience. But, one by one other leaders of the people joined him, and eventually, and incredibly, they persuaded the soldiers to feed and clothe the prisoners, put the weakest on donkeys and take them all back to Jericho, within easy reach of their own capital city, Jerusalem.

Good begins with individuals and small actions. Some small actions swell to significant movements. We have seen examples of this in the last week. We can be proud of our citizens. Led by our Prime Minister New Zealand has refused to accept violence and demonstrated on a huge scale that actions of love and kindness are the way to defeat evil. The world is taking notice and is impressed.

Discrimination happens all the time. People are treated badly for many reasons but mostly because they appear different in the eyes of their oppressors. Developing awareness and promoting understanding helps curb our ready inclination to think of any group as 'the other.' Jesus expressed it succinctly with, 'love your neighbour as yourself.'

True religions have at their core the Golden Rule. They believe what we believe. In true faith there is no them and us, there is only us. Doing great good, is the domain of great leaders, but no small action for good is ever wasted. Kia kaha.

*2 Chronicles 15:1-3 & 28:8-15*

# Argula von Grumbach (1492–1554)

On Reformer's Sunday sermons are preached to remind and inform listeners about men of faith who have taken bold stands against oppression. It is the day that the Church honours its forefathers.

We are so used to history being his-story that we become lulled into thinking that only males took bold and positive action against injustice. Of course, this is not how it was in any history, but the sad fact is that actions taken by females to reform systems seldom got recorded by historians. However, one influential female supporter of Martin Luther can be located in written records. It is up to us to give her story the place it deserves when celebrating reformers. I offer the following 'public information' to whet your appetite for discovering more about unsung females of faith.

Argula von Grumbach (née von Stauff) (1492–1554) was a Bavarian noblewoman who, from the 1520s, became involved in the Protestant Reformation debates going on in Germany. She is known as the first Protestant woman writer, publishing hundreds of letters and poems promoting and defending Martin Luther and his supporters. She is most known for directly challenging the University of Ingolstadt's faculty in a letter speaking out against the arrest of a Lutheran student. As one of the few women at the time openly speaking out her views, her writings sparked thousands of copies of her letters and poems circulating within a few years of their publication.

She was born Argula von Stauff in 1492 (the year 'Columbus sailed the ocean blue'). The von Stauff family lived in a castle were leaders among Bavarian nobility. Her upbringing was political and religious in a household where education was prized. When she was ten her father gave her a beautifully crafted Koberger Bible, despite the Franciscan preachers discouraging it, saying Scripture would "only confuse her."

At age of sixteen, Argula joined the court in Munich, becoming a lady-in-waiting to Queen Kunigunde, daughter of the Emperor Frederick III.

The Queen had a strong personality and was passionate about politics and religion. It is likely that in this environment Argula's Bible study became a serious endeavour.

When she was 24 Argula married Friedrich von Grumbach, and had four children, (George, Hans Georg, Gottfried and Apollonia). Friedrich died young and 3 years later she married Count von Schlick, but he died within two years. She was politically active during her marriages and critics called her called by many offensive epithets such as "shameless whore" and a "female desperad" and accused her of being a neglectful wife and mother, but she also had strong supporters. A Lutheran preacher wrote that she "knows more of the divine Word than all of the red hats (canon lawyers and cardinals) ever saw or could conceive of."

In the letter that made her famous, Argula cited over 80 Scriptures making comparisons against the behaviour of the university theologians. The letter was turned into a booklet and provoked a huge reaction, greatly angering the theologians. It became a bestseller with fourteen editions published in two months.

An excerpt from her letter…

> To the honourable, worthy, high-born, erudite, noble, stalwart Rector and all the Faculty of the University of Ingolstadt…
>
> …You seek to destroy all of Luther's works. In that case you will have to destroy the New Testament, which he has translated. In the German writings of Luther and Melanchthon I have found nothing heretical… Even if Luther should recant,what he has said would still be the Word of God. I would be willing to come and dispute with you in German…. You have the key of knowledge and you close the kingdom of heaven. But you are defeating yourselves. The news of what has been done to this lad of 18 has reached us and other cities in so short a time that soon it will be known to all the world. The Lord will forgive Arsacius, as he forgave Peter, who denied his master, though not threatened by prison and fire. Great good will yet come from this young man. I send you not a woman's ranting, but the Word of God. I write as a member of the Church of Christ against which the gates of hell shall not prevail…
>
> *Argula von Grumbach, 1523*

**Reference**

- https://en.wikipedia.org/wiki/Argula_von_Grumbach

# Susanna Wesley (1669–1742)

Susanna Wesley, nee Annesley, was a spirited and spiritual woman. Circumstances dictated a life of hardship, yet she remained a person of deep faith that earned her the title 'The Mother of Methodism.' The Methodist movement developed by sons John and Charles demonstrated to the unchurched poor of Britain that they were persons of value and possibly saved England from the bloody revolution experienced in France. Their mother's influence had a major impact on her sons and the Methodist movement could not have developed in the manner it did without her.

Susanna gave birth to 19 children but only ten survived to adulthood. Like their father, Rev Samuel Wesley, their three boys became ordained clerics in the Church of England. Most of the Wesley children were given Biblical names but the family used pet names for all of them except Charles. Their father was Rector of Epworth, a depressing village set in an island of swamp. Clerical appointments were known as a 'Living' but it was very difficult to make a living in this rough rural place. Many in the parish disliked their rector finding him too scholarly and inflexibly moral. His politics opposed those of the most influential man in the village who actively stirred up anti feelings.

Susanna's meticulously organized life revolved around her large household. She instilled habits of faith, discipline and respect. In a time when few girls received an education, she insisted her girls learn to read before they learn to work. Each of her children was taught the alphabet on their 5th birthday. Despite being continually pregnant for 20 years Susanna's rigorous 'methods' enabled the household to function through tragedy and poverty. As well as home-schooling all her children she scheduled time alone with each on a weekly basis.

Husband Samuel was often absent and of little practical use when present. Though devout he was hot-tempered and constantly in debt. During one of Samuel's long sojourns in London Susanna became so exasperated by the curate's preaching that she began Sunday afternoon prayer meetings for the household in her kitchen. The household included a maid and other help such as a children's nurse, gardener or handyman. The villagers heard of her meetings and some asked if they could attend. Numbers grew to around 30 in winter then climbed to over 200 in summer. The curate wrote a letter of complaint to Samuel, who wrote to Susanna demanding explanation. She replied explaining, 'These meetings are different ... they are not held in a church ... a woman is the leader but not a man among them is capable of reading a sermon ... if I was not using my talents in caring for these people I would be failing in my responsibilities.'

Susanna encouraged discussion and listened to concerns. Her actions brought a remarkable change to the villagers' attitude towards church and the Wesleys. Her self-discipline and methodical ways were inherited by her sons. When the children left home, Susanna kept in touch with copious letters.

In old age Susanna moved to London to support John in his great work. Her reproving of John for not recognising the value of lay people led him to train and commission lay preachers, that he called local preachers. Influenced by his mother John promoted female leadership in Methodist causes including the weekly class meetings that became a hallmark of the Methodist movement.

## Susanna (Annesley) Wesley – timeline...

Susanna's father, Dr Samuel Annesley was a distinguished scholar and clergyman, known as 'the St Paul of the Nonconformists.' He lived a comfortable life and his children were well educated and encouraged to discuss issues.

1669    20 January: Susanna was born, the 25th child of Dr Samuel Annesley and Mary (White) Annesley (2nd wife, the 1st wife died in childbirth).

1647    Mother died; Susanna aged 6 (only 6 of Mary's 24 children survived to adulthood).

1681    Aged 12 decided the customs of the Established Church of England was her religious preference. Her decision was respected.

1682    Met the poet Samuel Wesley at her sister Elizabeth's wedding; Susanna was 13, Samuel 20 and a friend of the groom; Samuel Wesley presented a poem in honour of the couple; Samuel became a frequent visitor to Susanna's home. They enjoyed discussing theology having both rejected the nonconformist faiths they had been brought up in, for the Church of England.

1688    Married Samuel Wesley; he showed more interest in his writing than in his wife.

| 1690 | Son, Samuel (Sammy) born at her father's house as they were living in 'mean lodgings' in Holborn; moved to a Living at South Ormsby, Lincolnshire four months later. |
|------|------|
| 1691 | Gave birth to a daughter at Ormsby who died within weeks. |
| 1692 | Gave birth to Emilia (Emily) at Ormsby. |
| 1694 | Gave birth to twin sons, Annesley & Jedidiah. They died within months. |

1694 Susanna feared Sammy was speech impaired, though he appeared to be intelligent he did not use words.

1695 Gave birth to a girl, Susanna (Sukey).

Sammy spoke for first time, the day before his 5th birthday, a complete sentence: "Here I am Mother." (Next day Susanna taught him the alphabet and within weeks Sammy could read the first chapter of Genesis).

1696 Mary (Molly) born; was dropped by her nurse body causing a permanent spinal deformity.

1667 Samuel dismissed from his chaplaincy for objecting to his patron's morals; was offered an accepted a Living as Rector of Epworth.

Father died.

Moved to Epworth with her husband, four children, and mother-in-law (a last minute decision by Samuel who feared his mother, Mary Wesley, may become destitute – how long she lived with them is not known).

Sister Elizabeth died.

Mehetabel (Hetty) born.

Emily began lessons.

Sammy started at the village school, left after a year.

1698 Another child was born and buried.

1669 Gave birth to premature twins, John & Benjamin, both died within a few months.

1701 Gave birth to twins, John Benjamin & Anne (Nancy); the boy died seven weeks later.

1702 Refused to say Amen to husband's prayer for the King; he left her bed, then the house; returned for a few days when the King died then went to London for months.

Rectory badly damaged by arson (soon after Samuel's return).

1703 26 June: Gave birth to John Benjamin (Jacky).

1704    Sammy, aged 14, went to Westminster School in London.

1705    Flax crop (much needed supplementary income) burnt by aggressive villagers.

Gave birth to another son – accidentally smothered by his nurse three weeks later.

Samuel sent to debtors' prison in Lincoln Castle.

Found their three cows wounded by stabbing, unable to provide milk.

Sent her rings to Samuel to pawn; knowing how much they meant to her he wouldn't, instead he wrote to the Archbishop of York, who had given financial help after the house fire. Archbishop Sharp visited (observing Susanna's courage, left some coins and cleared Samuel's debts, Samuel had been in prison for three months).

1706    8 May: Gave birth to Martha (Patty).

Hetty read the New Testament in Greek at age eight (she was a gifted child, intelligent, lively and attractive; in her teens aided Samuel with his scholarly work and attracted many suitors but none won her father's approval).

1707    18 December: Gave birth to Charles.

1708    09 February: Rectory set on fire. The children escaped through a ground floor window. Susanna aged 39, heavily pregnant with her 19th child had to force her way through thick smoke to the door and collapsed outside; a head count revealed 5 year old Jacky (John) was missing, onlookers saw him at an upstairs window, some men formed a human ladder and grabbed him just before the burning roof caved in; Samuel fell on his knees with a prayer of thanks. Susanna, quoted Zechariah 3:2, declaring, "Is not this a brand plucked out of the fire?" believing this child must have been saved for some special task.

With the house destroyed the children were dispersed among people who would have them Susanna and Emily boarded with a local family.

Keziah (Kezzy) was born in March.

1710    Family reunited in new rectory after a year of separation; within a few months Samuel returned to London leaving a curate to run the parish.

| 1711 | Five of the children got smallpox (nursed by Susanna, recovered without scaring). |
|---|---|
| | Began prayer meetings in kitchen (for household, also attended by locals). |
| 1714 | John aged 11 went to Charterhouse School, London. |
| 1715 | Sammy married Ursula Berry; Charles, aged eight, went to Westminster school. |
| 1716 | During the winter unexplained knockings, noises, and door openings began to occur in attic, along with varying visual manifestations. The girls named their ghost 'Old Jeffrey' after a recently deceased gardener; every member of the household including servants and guests experienced the phenomenon. Samuel was advised to leave the house, but he refused telling his daughters, "Two Christians are an overmatch for the devil," and to his clerical advisors replied, "Let the devil flee from me; I will never flee from the devil." Susanna, aware of her daughters disease counselled, "It is our wisdom and duty to prepare seriously for all events." The extraordinary events persisted over months. No explanations were found, 'Old Jeffrey' or the 'Epworth Poltergeist' remains one of the best documented ghosts in England. |
| 1717 | Sukey went to live with Uncle Samuel Annesley, he promised Sukey an expensive gift, and to his sister, Susanna 'an expectation.' Samuel Annesley departed for India. |
| 1718 | Sammy was ordained, having gained his M.A. |
| 1719 | Sukey married Richard Ellison (wealthy landowner but no gentleman). |
| 1720 | John entered Oxford on a Charterhouse scholarship. |
| | Emily went to live in London with Uncle Matthew Wesley, fell in love but not permitted to marry; couldn't find work, took up teaching in Lincolnshire. |
| 1724 | Parish of Wroot added to Samuel's Living (care) could only be reached by boat. Household moved to Wroot and run-down accommodation deciding to rent out the Epworth rectory enable sufficient income to cover their debts and their curate's allowance. |
| | Rented the rectory to Sukey and her husband who had money but treated her badly, Sukey had four children but it is not known if Susanna had much contact with her grandchildren. |

Susanna went to London (first time in 34 years), to meet her brother's ship, learns he has vanished along with his fortune.

1725    Household again went down with smallpox, not as severe as previously.

Hetty eloped (a disastrous marriage followed and permanent estrangement from her father).

Emily left Wroot, took a teaching position at a Lincoln girls' boarding school.

Kezzy joined Emily as a teacher in the same school.

1726    John elected as a Fellow of Lincoln College making his parents very proud.

1727    Samuel became twisted with rheumatism.

1728    John was ordained and took over Wroot curacy for two years.

1731    Sukey's husband moved his family out of the Rectory.

The Wesley's moved back to Epworth, now knowing Richard was violent to Sukey.

Uncle Matthew Wesley visited; took Patty back to London with him.

1732    Emily started her own school at Gainsborough.

1733    Samuel asked Sammy to take over his Living, Sammy refused.

1734    John refused to take over the Living.

Molly married Rev Johnny Whitelamb.

Samuel gave Johnny the Wroot Living.

Molly died within the year after giving birth to a stillborn child

Patty was secretly engaged to Westley Hall, a young clergyman (who had been in the Holy Club at Oxford and was a friend of John's). Unaware of this development John invited Westly to accompany him from London to visit Epworth; Kezzy was at home. Westly flirted with Kezzy and gave her a friendship ring.

1735    Patty married Westley Hall in London; Kezzy was inconsolable.

Samuel died (soon after completing his great work on Job).

Sukey left Richard, taking the children and hiding among friends in London.

Emily married Robert Harper.

John and Charles went to America as missionaries.

1736   Susanna and Kezzy lived with Emily then moved to Sammy's at Tiverton in Devon.

1737   Kezzy went to London to live with Patty and her husband. Susanna joined them when they shifted to Fisherton near Salisbury.

1738   Late in May John and Charles had conversion experiences at separate meetings in London that led to them forming the Methodist movement; Susanna took a keen interest.

Westley Hall deserted Patty and took his mistress to the West Indies.

1739   Sammy died aged 40 after a short illness, having been an usher at Westminster School for 20 years and Master of Blundell's School in Tiverton, for six years.

Took up residence at John's London center, The Foundery, and became involved in the Methodist cause.

Only ordained Anglican clergy were permitted to preach at the Foundery chapel. During a period when John and Charles were absent a lay person who had been reading the scriptures went to the pulpit and explain them; initially shocked Susanna liked what he had to say. When John discovered what had happened Susanna informed her son that she felt Mr Maxfield was as entitled to preach as he was, and John should hear for himself. He did and decided lay people could be useful in spreading the Gospel if trained as local preachers.

1740   Emily left her husband and joined her mother at the Foundery (and for 25 years did the work of a deaconess).

1741   Kezzy died aged 32.

1742   23 July: Susanna died aged 73 (a memorial to her stands in the grounds of the Foundery; she is buried nearby at Bunhill Fields nonconformist's cemetery, Islington).

Emily, Sukey, Hetty, Nancy, Patty and John gathered round Susanna's bed (Charles was in Wales and could not be contacted). Her last words were: "Children as soon as I am released sing a psalm of praise."

**References**

- *Susanna Wesley – A Radical in the Rectory,* by Marion Field; Highland Books UK, 1998

- *The Wesley Sisters,* by Frederick E Maser, Foundery Press UK, 1990

## One of Susanna's Prayers

From age 17 to her death at 73, Susanna spent one hour a day in prayer and meditation.

Morning and evening, I commit my soul to Jesus Christ, the saviour of the world. Enable me, O God, to observe what he saith unto me: resolutely to obey His precepts and endeavour to follow His example in those things wherein He is exhibited to us as a pattern for our imitation, make plain to me that no circumstance nor time of life can occur but I may find something either spoken by our Lord himself or by His spirit in the prophets or apostles that will direct my conduct, if I am but faithful to Thee and my own soul. Amen.

# Lenna Button (1901-1940)

**Female reader:**

29 August 1940

Dear Diary,

For the moment all is quiet. The men in my care are sleeping. My shift ends at dawn. It seems I may be granted a little time for myself. It is hard to believe I am here, me an Aussie in Kent wearing the uniform of the Women's Auxiliary Air Force. I thought the 'Great War' was meant to end all wars! I came to England to study, not to join the WAAFs. I only meant to be a religious sister, a deaconess, not an untrained nursing sister.

As a youngster I never thought of travelling. My thoughts were like other girls, marriage and children. But after four years working in the North Melbourne Mission, I understood that service to others was my ambition. That's why I went to Christchurch, NZ, to train as a Deaconess. They were great days; such fun we girls had living together in that big house in Latimer Square. They called me 'Buttons' and my best friend, Rita Snowden, was 'Snowie.' Love of God and desire to serve was a strong bond. We formed lasting friendships. I'm writing this now because of Rita. She said we should all write our stories. 'People live stories, people need stories to live.' If only I could write like her!

Snowie is so creative. The New Zealand Deaconess badge was her idea, but she invited my input. We came up with two interlocking triangles, the points representing the three persons of the trinity and the three theological virtues of faith hope and charity, to complement our motto Non Sibi; Sed Aliis – Not for self but for others.

What a privilege it is to be able to help others. My first posting at St Albans, Christchurch gave wonderful opportunity to work with youth. I particularly enjoyed Guides, but some of the girls came from very poor homes. My concern led me to a meeting organised by Cora Wilding. Cora was a Christchurch physiotherapist who had been to Britain to study the health benefits of fresh air and sunshine. She had established the New Zealand branch of the Sunshine League. The meeting was to encourage charities to organise Sunshine Camps. The camp concept not a new idea, the work of Dr Gunn was well known in New Zealand. Elizabeth Gunn was a Wanganui school doctor who organised camps for undernourished children during the war. Sunshine Camps made sound sense to me. I saw this was something I could do. My parish was very supportive, and I ran several camps in the Christchurch area. The camps made a real difference to some children, but our efforts were a mere cheering droplet in an ocean of anxiety.

I was transferred to Dunedin in 1932 when the Depression was at its height. In my work with the District Nurse I saw first-hand the terrible effects of poverty. I discussed it with my boss, Mission Superintendent, Rev Leslie Neale, and discovered he was a firm believer in the work of Sunshine Camps. He had actually met Dr Elizabeth Gunn while working as an army chaplain during the Great War. Leslie said Dr Gunn was a bit of a character – voice like a Sergeant Major, quite intimidating, but passionate about the physical and moral welfare of children. She ran her children's camps with military discipline, 'Gunn, Gospel and Grub' the media called it, but she got results!

Rev Neale proposed buying land for the express purpose of a health camp. His vision was to extend the children's camp idea to also cater for needy women. It was an exciting concept. In November he bought a cottage on the Otago Peninsula in a wonderfully scenic spot, an ideal site for a camp. It was quite near Mr Lanarch's stately home – the place everyone called a The Castle, but Mr Larnach had named it The Camp. We must be onto something, I thought, when I made the connection. However, the Mission Board was peeved that Leslie had made the purchase without consulting them and refused to reimburse him. He decided to go ahead anyway. I could have hugged him. He retained ownership and together we sought donations to renovate the cottage. With tents we could accommodate up to 40 at a time. That first summer 180 mothers and children passed through our camps and Leslie dreamed of acquiring further property and building permanent accommodation.

The actual camps were my responsibility. I organised a programme of health-giving routines – good food, plenty of fresh-air, exercise, sleep and spiritual nourishment. Some of the children had never used a toothbrush before. Toothbrush drill became an exercise they took pride in, along with physical jerks and bed-making. Many came from undisciplined backgrounds and a set bedtime was quite new to them. We allowed plenty of time for games and nature rambles. Swimming in the sea was a real highlight. Most of our country children had not so much as paddled in the sea. With my wonderful volunteers we saw to it that the children ate meat, fresh fruit and vegetables every day, along with a pint of milk. We gave careful attention to their moral and spiritual wellbeing. Many had scant acquaintance with Bible stories and Christian standards. Our aim was 'to broadcast everything of pure refreshment and delight.' Watching the children blossom was a real joy.

The Government had noticed the good work of the Sunshine Camps and was providing financial aid through the sale of health stamps, but only to non-sectarian camps. Ours was considered sectarian. It was so unfair! We had never restricted our intake to Methodists. When challenged they said our camps did not fulfil the criteria as we used our building to also care for adults. Leslie was so committed to the task he applied for a grant from the 1933 Great Easter Art union. It caused a terrible furore in church circles, but he maintained the ends justified the means. Many public figures supported him, but the Church felt nothing could sanctify 'tainted money' and Leslie was compelled to refuse the grant. But now the Mission Board was on our side. Leslie and I put our efforts into radio appeals. We had our own radio programme *The Church of the Helping Hand*. Our project captured the imagination of the city. Games, sports equipment and other goods came pouring in. I felt like a bride receiving wedding gifts. We attracted a tremendous number of small monetary donations plus a few really large ones from influential people, and we even got a health stamp grant. In 1936 I joined the newly formed National Federation of Health Camps. So much more can be achieved when people work together.

Our new complex was designed by an architect and was quite splendid. I described the progress to my listeners. "Every child will have a single bed, a delight to little people who are in the habit of sharing with two or three other members of the family – a wardrobe, a bedside table and a colour scheme that will write its own story in the child's book of memories." The Prime Minister, Michael Joseph Savage, had a preview of the near finished buildings and he was most impressed by the substantial brick buildings, spacious accommodation and wonderful play areas.

I'll never forget Saturday March 13th, 1937 – over 2,000 people came to the opening. They came by car and bus and boat. The Peninsular was swarming with people. It was claimed that no other health institution in

NZ could compare to the Company Bay Health Home. It was a pinnacle of achievement, but in June I was transferred to the Auckland Mission.

I can hear the sound of aircraft. What is it with men that drives them to destruction? Can't they see war is never an answer! I've seen fine young men mutilated by terrible wounds. At least they made it back. So many families have lost brothers, sons, fathers… It is not only men caught up in this madness, civilians are targeted in their homes. Beautiful Kent, 'the garden of England' is becoming a landscape of craters.

The men in my care are mostly sick with common illnesses but some are recovering from injuries. I have some nasty burns to tend, and cuts, I've learnt to suture. But the men don't come to my sickbay just to have their wounds dressed. Many come for a listening ear. They need someone to share their fears with. Some of them are mere boys. Those with permanent injuries wonder if they will be employable when the war is over. Some have disfiguring burns and doubt that their sweethearts will still love them. Others worry about their children and what separation does to relationships. It would be easy to get downhearted, but I am determined to remain optimistic. These courageous airmen deserve the sight of a cheerful face. My name helps, Edna Lenna Button. 'Sister Lenna, bright as a button,' they quip. The siren! Must go…

**Male reader:**

'An air raid came upon us very suddenly and we were all running to take shelter. She had got all her patients from the sickbay into the trench and was following them in when a huge bomb fell very near and she was caught in the blast. Her death was instantaneous…You have every reason to be proud of her, for not only did she do her duty during the last days of her life, but in all the difficult days preceding; she was full of quiet, cheerful encouragement which she radiated to us all.

*Corporal M M Willis, R A F. Station, Biggin Hill, Kent*

*Extract from a letter to Sister Rita Snowden*

## References

- *Not Self – But Others* – Wesley A. Chambers, 1987
- Leslie Bourneman Neale – *A Man of Faith and Vision* – Leah Taylor, 2000

**Presentation suggestions**

Begin with 'The Deaconess Hymn' Methodist Hymnbook 786 – Lord, grant us like the watching five…

*Sister Lenna* wears a nursing veil and reads from the lectern, or sits at small table as if writing, and uses a lapel microphone.

To add drama, play a siren sound, followed by silence, then a male voice reading the extract from the letter.

# Ann Turner (1798–1893)

I can scarce believe that I have reached the great age of 95 years knowing that I have given birth to 15 children 12 of whom reached adulthood. My dear children have helped sweeten a widowhood of 29 years … but for 40 years my husband and I served God on Wesleyan mission stations. We began our work in the most remote mission station in the world on the east coast of New Zealand. We also served in Tonga and Fiji. My talented husband had the privilege of developing a written language for the Tongan people. We spent time in Hobart and returned to New Zealand in 1836 and worked in the well-established mission on the Hokianga harbour where ships plied the timber trade. Three years later we moved to Australia with ten of our children and worked in Tasmania, Sydney and Brisbane, where I buried my dear Nathaniel.

I can't remember how long I've been down here at Kew in Victoria. Much to my delight this town has a secondary school for girls, the Methodist Ladies College. It was the wonderful Rev William Fitchett who convinced the Methodist Conference that girls need as good an education as boys. He opened this excellent boarding and day school, about ten years ago. I feel sure it will become one of Australia's very best schools … But I've got off the subject, sorry … I tend to do that these days. You wanted to hear about my life. After such a long a life it is my early memories that return with the greatest clarity.

Growing up as I did on a small farm in Staffordshire, I had no concept of the vast wild world and the adventures that were possible for a simple milkmaid. The handsome fellow who swept me off my feet was Anglican by birth but as a young adult had experienced a strong calling to be a Wesleyan missionary to the South Seas. I married Nathaniel Turner at Stoke-on-Trent on the 10th of January 1822. He was ordained a Methodist minister in London not two weeks later, on the 23rd of January. What a whirlwind time that was. We were to depart our native land the very next month. Nathaniel was full of excitement, but his situation was quite different from mine. He had been orphaned at the tender age of nine years. As for myself I had lived in a close family setting for all of my 24 years. My excitement was greatly tempered by the anguish of knowing I may never see any of them again.

But I loved my husband and shared his steadfast belief that we were doing God's work.

The Reverend William White was our mentor and companion when we boarded the *Deveron* bound for Hobart, Tasmania. He was a person of unpredictable temperament. The long sea journey took an arduous four months. Our baby girl was born less than nine months later. Nathaniel insisted she be given my maiden name and thus my parents would be ever remembered through her. Baby Ann was only 3 months old when we boarded the *Brampton* and set sail for New Zealand.

This journey was very different to our former voyage. We were in the company of Reverend Samuel Marsden, and also Rev Henry Williams with his wife Marianne and their three young children, such a lovely Anglican family, as were the Fairiburns with their two young ones. Sarah Fairburn was pregnant with her third. William Fairburn was a carpenter and they were returning to the Anglican mission. It was so good being able to talk with Sarah who knew what life was like in Maoriland. The other Wesleyan worker, John Hobbs was also a carpenter, though later we discovered he could turn his hand to almost any skill, and we had a young servant girl Betsy. With such good company how could we not be filled with great excitement and high hopes of bringing the love of Jesus to a county of people who did not know Christ.

Alas it was not as easy as we had thought. To be honest working with Maori was difficult and we had much cause to be discouraged. But in those early days the Anglicans of the Church Missionary Society were a wonderful support to us Wesleyans. We women formed lifelong friendships. I admit it was bleak living at Kaeo in the mission the Leighs had named Wesleydale. I had expected to have the company of Catherine Leigh, but her husband Samuel was so ill they left for Australia on the ship that delivered us to this far flung shore. Apart from 14 year old Betsy I was the only white woman at Kaeo. Betsy went back to Australia the following year. None the less I was able to engage with some Maori women and girls. I taught them how to sew, though they did complain that the needles bit their fingers. As time went on, we learned more of each other's languages and I was able to teach some of the girls and boys how to write English words. But it was a very pleasant surprise when Mrs Wade arrived at Wesleydale in 1827. Mrs Wade was the wife of Luke Wade, an ex-sailor who had been employed as a labourer by the CMS and had come to work for us. This unexpected situation was almost comical, poor Luke had no way of knowing his wife was making her own way to New Zealand and he had left for England to get her as soon as he had secured a suitable dwelling.

With no female company the men had felt able to delight in my darling children. Little Ann was such a bright child ... she prattled away in the native tongue from the age of two. I gave birth every year we served at Wesleydale. My CMS friends were of great support, but even so I lost two sons. One by miscarriage but the death of wee Nathaniel at 11 months was the hardest trial I ever had to bear. His loss affected us all. John Hobbs was so impacted he spent weeks carving an elaborate mock iron fence to surround the little grave, but my husband felt it may convey an inappropriate message of superiority to the natives.

A most distressing thing happened ... they tried to keep it from me, but I leaned from a native woman that Nathaniel junior's dear little body had been disturbed for the blanket it had been wrapped in. I could have given up there and then had I not been a woman of faith. I took comfort by the thought of our loved son in the arms of our Saviour.

Our wee John Sargent was just five weeks old when the great disaster happened. We had become aware of unrest among the tribes. The warrior chief Hongi Hika wanted to take control of the Whangaroa. Missionaries had been promised protection but with war in the air this was less certain than before. One day we heard the chilling sound of angry warriors approaching. Then one appeared at our doorway. I rushed to bolt the door but was not quick enough. A tall warrior had entered. He raised his weapon to strike me but miraculously his club struck a shelf containing a jar of nails. They poured down on him and the man was so startled that he ran away.

Our men grabbed the small children and we fled through our cornfield to the track that led towards the Anglican mission, but it started to rain so we took shelter in the bush. Mrs Wade kept tripping over her wet skirt and the children were shivering. We had travelled bout two kilometres when we encountered three Maori that we knew to be from our valley. They urged us to wait but our men feared these Maori could no longer be trusted. Sit on that hill, they instructed. It was clear to me that we would be in full view of any approaching war party.

"Our cause is an honourable one, therefore let us go forward," I declared with confidence. Much to the distress of the mission's Maori children our men rose and led us back to the track. John Hobbs reminded them to trust the Lord for he had promised to be with those who served him. We came across a friendly native who agree to lead us. After crossing the river twice, we encountered the terrifying sight of possibly 300 men armed with muskets and hatchets. They were headed by chief Patuaone. He had impressive control of his men. The formidable company halted on his command. His chiefs and our men pressed noses in the traditional manner. Patuaone then bade us all to kneel. We did not know if we would ever rise again but his chiefs formed a circle around us, and the fighting men were ordered away. Patuone raised his hands over us and dismissed us with the words, "Haere atu kotu ... Go ye onward."

Patuone was a chief of great mana. When he was young his father had placed a blessing on him with the words, "He Tangata pai koe, mau e hohou I te ronga ... you will be a good man a peacemaker." It was on land controlled by him and his brother Waka Nene's that three years later a Wesleyan mission was re-established in the Hokianga.

I have often reflected had it not been for the grace of God extended to us on that fateful day we all would have died and ten of our children would never have been born. I would not have reached age 29 yet here I am safe among family in the fine antipodean town of Kew praising God for 95 event filled years.

## References

- *John Hobbs,* by T. M. I. Williment, V. R. Ward. Government Printer Wellington NZ 1985.

- https://www.findagrave.com

- https://trove.nla.gov.au/newspaper/article/155399774

# Bible Queens and Kings

The word 'king' appears in the Bible more than 3,000 times, the word 'queen' about 80 times. Kings feature in dominant roles, but most biblical queens get only an incidental mention. To the chroniclers of the time the most important role of queens was to provide sons to continue the dynasty.

## The United Kingdom

According to the Biblical account, after allocating tribal land to the descendants of Jacob the Tribes of Israel lived as a confederation under ad hoc charismatic leaders called judges. Around 1020 BCE, under threat from foreign peoples, the tribes decided to band together under the rule of a king forming what is now called the United Kingdom of Israel. The prophet Samuel anointed Saul from the Tribe of Benjamin as the first king. He was not succeeded by his son.

**House of Saul**   c. 1020–1003 BCE.

**House of David**  c. 1003–970 BCE.
Jerusalem the capital of Israel
**Solomon** (c. 970–930 BCE)
**Rehoboam** (c. 930–915 BCE)

When Rehoboam had reigned three years, the Hebrew Kingdom divided into two kingdoms.

**Israel**, the northern kingdom was ruled by a series of dynasties beginning with Jeroboam. Its first capital city was Shechem, then Tirza, and finally Samaria.

**Judah**, the southern kingdom retained Jerusalem as its capital city and was ruled by the House of David for a further 340 years.

The Neo-Assyrian Empire conquered and destroyed the northern kingdom of Israel in 722 BCE. The southern kingdom of Judah fell in 586 BCE. Many of the people were taken to Babylon. This period of Jewish history is known as the Exile. After the return from Exile the temple was rebuilt but the kingdoms were not re-established.

### Hebrew Queens

Abigail, Abihail/Abi, Abijah/Abijam, Abital, Ahinoam, Athaliah, Azuba, Bathsheba, Basemath, Eglah, Hadassah, Haggith, Hamutal, Hephzibah, Hoglah, Jecholiah, Jedidah, Jehoaddan, Jerusha, Jezebel, Maacah, Meshullemeth, Michal, Naamah, Nehushta, Taphath, Zibiah, Zeruah

Lists of the Hebrew Kings are plentiful. Lists of Hebrew Queens are not.

Identifying the wives of the kings is difficult. Some reasons being: kings tended to have children by more than one woman; exactly who fulfilled the function of Queen is often not clear; or important, in the Hebrew records. However, the official recorders, of David's dynasty, named several wives though were more interested in noting who the king's mother was. The northern record keepers made no effort to record queens. They found it difficult enough keeping track of their kings.

The only Hebrew woman to reign as Queen was **Athaliah**, a princess from the northern kingdom who married a southern king, King Jehoram. Athalia seized his throne after he was killed and succeeded in keeping it by ensuring the death of other contenders. However, Jehoram's sister, **Jehosheba**, managed to save the King's youngest son, baby Joash. She kept him hidden until aged 7 when he was legally able to occupy the throne. Another woman who merits mention in connection to royalty is the prophetess **Huldah**. King Josiah had his officials consult her in regard to what religious duties God required of the people.

Some Bible characters, particularly leaders, are confusingly called by more than one name and spellings of one name may differ, particularly between the King James Version and later translations. Kings are listed in order. Queens are listed in bold print.

| | |
|---|---|
| **Saul** | **Ahinoam**, *1 Samuel 14:50* |
| | **Rizpah** concubine of Saul, *2 Samuel 3:7* (Guards the bodies of her sons, *2 Samuel 21:8-11*) |
| **David** | **Michal** younger daughter of King Saul, no offspring (other wives named in *2 Samuel 3:3-5*) |
| | **Ahinoam** mother of Amnon |
| | **Abigail** mother of Chileab |
| | **Maacah** mother of Absalom |
| | **Abital** mother of Sephatah |
| | **Haggith** mother of Adonijah |
| | **Eglah** mother of Ithream |
| | **Bathsheba** mother of Jedidiah (Solomon), *2 Samuel 12:24* |

| Solomon | **Naamah** mother of Rehoboam, *1 Kings 14:21, 31*; plus, many other wives |
| | **Taphath** a daughter of Solomon, *1 Kings 4:11* |
| | **Basemath** a daughter of Solomon, *1 Kings 4:15* wife of Ahimaaz. |

## The Southern Kingdom of Judah

| Kings | (Reign BCE) | Queens |
| --- | --- | --- |
| Rehoboam | (930–913) | **Maacah** mother of Abijam (Abijah), *1 Kings 15:2* |
| Abijam | (913–910) | 14 wives, 22 sons, 16 daughters, *2 Chronicles 13:21* |
| Asa | (910–870) | **Azuba** mother of Jehoshaphat, *1 Kings 22:42* |
| Jehoshaphat | (870–853) | Eventful reign; no mention of wife, succeeded by son |
| Jehoram | (853–841) | **Athaliah** daughter of Ahab & Jezebel, *2 Kings 8:18*, mother of Ahaziah |
| Ahaziah / Uzziah | (841–840) | **Zibiah** mother of Joash, *2 Kings 12:1* |
| **Athaliah** | (840–836) | Ruled until replaced by Ahaziah's 7-year-old son, Joash |
| Joash | (836–796) | **Jehoaddan** mother of Amaziah, *2 Kings 14:2* |
| Amaziah | (796–767) | **Jecholiah** mother of Azariah, *2 Kings 15:2* |
| Azariah | (767–750) | **Jerusha** daughter of Zadok, mother of Jotham, *2 Kings 15:33* |
| Jotham | (750–735) | Affected by leprosy, deposed by son Ahaz |
| Ahaz | 735–727) | **Abi** mother of Hezekiah daughter of Zechariah, *2 Chronicles 29:1* |
| Hezekiah | (728-696) | **Hephzibah** mother of Manasseh, *2 Kings 21:1* |
| Manasseh | (696-642) | **Meshullemeth**, mother of Amon, *2 Kings 21:19* |

| | | |
|---|---|---|
| Amon | (642–640) | **Jedidah** mother of Josiah, *2 Kings 21:1* |
| Josiah | (640–609) | **Zebidah** *2 Kings 23:36*; Hamutal mother of Jehoahaz, *2 Kings 23:31* |
| Jehoahaz | (609) | **Nehushta** mother of Jehoiakim, *2 Kings 24:68* |
| Jehoiakim | (609–598) | Captured by Nebuchadnezzar, taken to Babylon |
| Jehoiachin | (598–97) | **Hamutal** mother of Zedekiah, daughter of Jeremiah, *2 Kings 24:18* |
| Zedekiah | (597–586) | Uncle of Jehoiachin; taken by Nebuchadnezzar to Babylon |

## The Northern Kingdom of Israel

| Kings | (Reign BCE) | Queens |
|---|---|---|
| | | **Zeruah** wife of Nebat, mother of Jeroboam |
| Jeroboam | (930–909) | **Maacah,** *1 Kings 15:2*; Zeruah mother of Jeroboam, *1 Kings 11:26* |
| Nadab | (909–908) | Son of Jeroboam |
| Baasha | (908–885) | Son of Ahijah, of the house of Issachar |
| Elah | (885–884) | Son of Baasha |
| Zimri | (884) | Zimri killed Elah and his family |
| Tibni | (884–880) | Omri, commander of the army killed Zimri |
| Omri | (884–873) | Some people followed Omri, others Tibni, until defeated by Omri |
| Ahab | (873–853) | **Jezebel** daughter of King Ethbaal of Sidonia, *2 Kings 16:3* |
| Ahaziah | (853–852) | **Zibiah** mother of Joash, *2 Kings 12:1*; **Athaliah** mother of Ahaziah, *2 Kings 8:26* |
| Joram | (852–841) | Son of Ahab |
| Jehu | (841–813) | Commander of the army, assassinated Joram with an arrow |
| Jehoahaz | (813–798) | Son of Jehu |
| Jehoash | (798–781) | Son of Jehoahaz |
| Jeroboam II | (792–753) | Son of Jehoash |

| Zechariah | (753–752) | Son of Jeroboam II |
| Shallum | (752, 1 month) | Assassinated Zechariah |
| Menahem | (752–741) | Assassinated Shallum |
| Pekahiah | (741–739) | Son of Menahem |
| Pekah | (739–731) | Assassinated Pekanhiah |
| Hoshea | (731–722) | Assassinated Pekah; Israelites exiled to Assyria |

## Other Bible Queens

- **Mehetabel** – wife of Hadad, King of Edom, *Genesis 36-39*
- **Queen of Sheba** – identified as 'Nikauli' by historian Josephus, *1 Kings 10:1-13*
- **Tahpenes** – wife of Pharaoh – during reigns of David and Solomon, *1 Kings 11:19*
- **Vashti** and **Esther** – wives of King Ahaserus of Persia, *Esther 1:9, 2:17*
- **Herodias** – wife of Herod Agrippa 1, *Matthew 14:1-12*
- **Candace** Queen of Ethiopia, *Acts 8:27*
- **Bernice** sister/consort of King Agrippa 11, *Acts 25:13*

## Other women of royal connection

- **Merab** – elder daughter of Saul
- **Michal** – younger daughter of Saul; David's first wife
- **Tamar** [2] – daughter of David and Maacah, *2 Samuel 13:1*
- **Tamar** [3] – daughter of Absalom, *2 Samuel 14:27*
- **Abigail** [2] – sister of David; mother of Amasa, *2 Samuel 17:25*
- **Abishag** – concubine of David, *1 Kings 1:3*
- **Jehosheba** – sister of Jehoram, *2 Kings 11:2*
- **Bithiah** – a Pharaoh's daughter in the Judges period m. Mered, descendent of Judah, *1 Chronicles 4:18*

# Alphabet of Bible Women

**A**    Abigail, Abishag, Adah, Achsah, Anna, Apphia, Asenath, Athaliah

**B**    Basemath, Bathsheba, Bernice, Bilhah, Bithiah

**C**    Candace, Chloe, Claudia, Cozbi

**D**    Damaris, Deborah, Delilah, Dinah, Dorcas, Drusilla

**E**    Elisheba, Elizabeth, Esther, Eunice, Euodia, Eve

**F**    Felix's wife - Drusilla

**G**    Gomer, 'Good woman' (Proverbs 31)

**H**    Hagar, Haggith, Hannah, Hephzibah, Herodias, Hoglah, Huldah

**I**    Iscah (sister of Lot)

**J**    Jael, Jemimah, Jezebel, Joanna, Jochebed, Judith, Julia, Junias

**K**    Keren-happuch, Keturah, Keziah

**L**    Leah, Lilith, Lois, Lydia

**M**    Maacah, Mahlah, Martha, Mary, Mehetabel, Merab, Michal, Milchah, Miriam

**N**    Naamah, Naomi, Nehushta, Noah, Noadiah, Nympha

**O**    Olympas, Orpah

**P**    Peninnah, Persis, Phoebe, Priscilla / Prisca, Puah

**Q**    Queen Athaliah. Queen Esther, Queen of Sheba

**R**    Rachel, Rahab, Rebekah, Reumah, Rhoda, Rizpah, Ruth

**S**    Salome, Sapphira, Sarah / Sarai, Serah, Sheerah, Shiphrah, Susanna, Syntyche

**T**    Tabitha, Tamar, Tahpenes, Taphath, Tirzah, Tryphena, Tryphosa,

**U**    Uriah's wife, Bathsheba

**V**    Vashti (1st wife of King Ahasuerus / Xerxes)

**W**    Widow of Zarephath, Widow of Nain, Wise Woman

**X**    Xmas (associate with 'Mary')

**Y**    Young Woman (accused Peter)

**Z**    Zebidah, Zeresh, Zillah, Zilpah, Zipporah

# Alphabet of Bible Men

A    Aaron, Abednego, Abel, Abraham, Absalom, Adam, Agrippa, Ahab, Amon, Amos, Andrew, Apollos, Aquila, Asa, Asher

B    Balaam, Balak, Barak, Barabbas, Barnabas, Bartholomew, Bartimaeus, Belshazzar, Benjamin, Bethuel, Bildad, Boaz

C    Caiaphas, Cain, Caleb, Chuza, Clement, Cleopas, Cladius, Cornelius, Cush, Cyrus

D    Damarius, Dan, Daniel, Darius, David, Demetrius

E    Ehud, Eli, Elijah, Eliezar, Eliphaz, Elisha, Elkanah, Enoch, Ephraim, Esau, Eutychus, Ezekiel, Ezra

F    Felix, Festus, Fortunatus

G    Gabriel, Gad, Gamaliel, Gehazi, Gershom, Gideon, Goliath

H    Ham, Haman, Harbona, Haran, Hegai, Herod, Hezekiah, Hosea

I    Isaac, Isaiah, Ishmael, Israel, Issachar

J    Jabal, Jacob, Jairus, James, Jehu, Jephthah, Jeremiah, Jeroboam, Jesse, Jesus, Job, John, Jonah, Jonathan, Joseph, Joshua, Josiah, Jubal, Judah, Judas

K    Kish, Kenaz, King David...

L    Laban, Lamech, Lappidoth, Lazarus, Levi, Linus, Lot, Luke

M    Mark, Matthew, Mattahias, Mordecai, Methuselah, Mica, Moses

N    Naaman, Nabal, Naboth, Naphtali, Nathan, Nathaniel, Nebuchadnezzar, Nehemiah, Nicodemus, Noah, Nun

O    Obed, Obadiah, Oded, Omri, Onesimus, Othniel, Olympas

P    Paul, Perez, Peter, Pharaoh, Philemon, Philip, Pilate, Potiphar

Q    Quirinius, Quartus

R    Rehoboam, Reuben, Rameses, Rufus

S    Samson, Samuel, Saul, Seth, Silas, Simon, Simeon, Solomon

T    Terah, Thaddaeus, Theophilus, Timothy, Titus, Thomas

U    Uriah, Uriel, Uz, Uzziah

V    Vophsi (grandson of Naphtali spy), Vaizatha (son of Haman)

W    Warriors, Wild man, Wise Men

X    Xerxes

Y    Young man (who fell from window, Eutychus)

Z    Zacchaeus, Zebedee, Zebulun, Zechariah, Zelophehad

# Bible names in Māori

| **Female** | | **Male** | |
|---|---|---|---|
| Angel | Anahera | Abel | Apera |
| Anna / Ann | Ana / Ani | Abraham | Āperahama |
| Bernice | Pereniki | Adam | Ārama |
| Bethany | Petani | Andrew | Ānaru |
| Claudia | Karauria | Benjamin | Pineāmine |
| Deborah | Tēpora | Caleb | Karepe |
| Diana | Raiana | Daniel | Ramiera |
| Dorcas | Roka | David | Rāwiri |
| Drusilla | Ruruhira | Elijah | Eria |
| Elizabeth | Erihapeti | Felix | Pirika |
| Esther | Ehetere | Isaac | Īhaka |
| Eunice | Unihi | Israel | Iharairia |
| Eve | Iwa | Jacob | Hākopa |
| Hannah | Hana | James | Hēmi |
| Josephine | Hohipine | Joseph | Hōhepa |
| Judith | Hutita/Iuriti | John | Hone |
| Julia | Hūria | Jonah | Hona |
| Leah | Rea | Joshua | Hōhua |
| Lois | Roihi | Luke | Ruku |
| Love | Aroha | Mark | Māka |
| Lydia | Riria | Matthew | Matiu |
| Martha | Maata | Michael | Mikaere |
| Mary | Mere/Meri | Moses | Mohi |
| Miriam | Miriama | Nathan | Nātana |
| Pauline | Pōrina | Noah | Noa |
| Phebe | Pipi | Paul | Pāora |
| Priscilla | Pirihira | Peter | Pētera |
| Rachel | Rāhera | Philip | Piripi |
| Rebecca | Rīpeka | Samuel | Hāmiora |
| Ruth | Rūta | Simon | Haimona |
| Sarah | Hera | Stephen | Tipene |
| Susanna | Hūhana | Thomas | Tāmati |
| Tabitha | Tapita | Timothy | Tīmoti |

# Bible names in latter days

**A**  Abigail Adams – 2nd USA First Lady; b. 1774

Anna Jarvis – US campaigner for Mother's Day; b. 1864

Anna Mary Robertson Moses – US folk artist known as 'Grandma Moses'; b. 1860

Anna Paquin – actress raised in Wellington; b. 1982

Abel Janszoon Tasman – Dutch seafarer and explorer; b. 1603

Abraham Lincoln – US President (1861–65); b. 1809

Adam Smith – Scottish philosopher, 'the Father of Economics'; b. 1723

Alexander Graham Bell – inventor of the telephone; b. 1847.

Andrew Carnegie – philanthropist, particularly noted for funding libraries; b. 1835

Andrew Lloyd Webber – musician, particularly for shows; b. 1948

Aaron Cruden – All Black 2010

Andrew Ellis – All Black 2006

Asa Chandler – established the Coca-Cola Company; b. 1851

**B**  Bathsheba (Brown) Marsden – mother of Rev Samuel Marsden; b. 1733

Barack Obama – 1st black President of USA, 2009-17; b. 1961

Benjamin Franklin – colonial American leader; b. 1775

Benjamin Britten – British classical composer; b. 1913

Benjamin Disraeli – British politician, served twice as PM; b. 1804

**C**  Claudia Orange – NZ historian, *The Treaty of Waitangi* 1987; b. 1938: (2 Timothy 4:21)

Chloe – a French fashion house founded in 1952

Caleb Ralph – All Black 1997

Clement Atlee – British PM from 1945 to 1951; b. 1883 (Philippians 4:3)

Clement Clark Moore – wrote poem *A Visit from St Nicholas* (1823); b. 1779

**D**  Deborah Kerr – Scottish born actress, played Anna in *The King and I*; b. 1921

Dorcas – dressmaker pins, made in Birmingham used in NZ from the 1950s

Dan Carter – All Black 2003

Daniel Boone – American hunter, trapper and explorer; b. 1734

David Fagan – Te Kuiti sheep shearer, won Golden Shears 16 times; b. 1961

David Hill – author, particularly young adult fiction; b. 1942

David Lange – Labour PM 1984 to 1989; cutting wit reputation; b. 1942

**E** Elizabeth Kubler-Ross – Swiss-born, American doctor, author of *On Death and Dying*, 1969; b. 1926

Elizabeth II – Queen of England; longest serving European monarch; b. 1926

Esther Williams – 'Hollywood's Mermaid', competitive swimmer and actress; b. 1921

Eunice Kennedy Shriver – founder of the Special Olympics; b. 1921

Ebenezer Scrooge – Dicken's character, *A Christmas Carol* published 1843

Eli Witney – inventor of the cotton gin; b. 1765

Elijah Wood – US actor played Frodo Baggins; b. 1981

**F** Felix Mendelssohn – German composer, symphonies and piano music; b. 1809

**G** Gabriel Fahrenheit – German scientist, invented the mercury-in-glass thermometer; b. 1686

Gideon Smales – Wesleyan missionary; b. 1888

**H** Hephzibah Lawry (nee Forsaith) – Wesleyan missionary in NZ, b. 1824

Hosea Gear – All Black 2008

**I** Isaac Newton – English physicist, formulated laws on motion; b. 1643

Isaac Merrett Singer – American inventor, Singer Sewing Machine; b. 1811

Isaiah Toeava – All Black 2005

Israel Dagg – All Black 2010

**J** Jemima Puddle-Duck – Beatrix Potter character, published 1905

Joanna Lumley – English comedy actress; b. 1946

Judith Medlicott – lawyer, and Chancellor of Otago University (1993–1998); b. 1950s

Julia Roberts – American actress and producer; b. 1967

Jacob Rothschild – British investment banker worth $5 billion; b. 1936

James K Baxter – NZ poet; b. 1926

James Cook – British explorer; b. 1773

James Watt – inventor of the steam engine; b. 1736

Jason O'Halloran – All Black 2000

Jeremiah (Jerry) Mateparae – Governor General of NZ, 2011-16; b. 1954

Jesse James – famous American outlaw; b. 1847

Joachim Albertini – Italian-born composer, famous opera 'Don Juan'; b. 1748

Joachim Christian Andersen, Danish professional footballer; b. 1966

Jethro Tull – successful British rock band, active 1967-2012

Jonah Lomu – Al Black 1994, attended Wesley College; b. 1975

John Bunyan – author of *The Pilgrim's Progress*; b. 1629

John Robert Godley – Irish statesman called 'Founder of NZ province of Canterbury'; b. 1814

John Hobbs – Wesleyan missionary; b. 1800

John Wayne – hero of Western movies; b. 1907

Jonathan Swift – British clergyman, satirist and author; wrote *Gulliver's Travels*; b. 1667

Joseph Haydn – Austrian composer; 'Father of the Symphony'; b. 1732

Joseph Lister – English scientist, pioneered antiseptics; b. 1827

Joseph Parker – NZ boxer, world heavyweight title 2016; b. 1992

Joshua Reynolds – English portrait painter; b. 1723:

Josiah Wedgewood – English pottery; b. 1730

Julius Vogel – London born Jew, 8th Premier of NZ 1873-76; founded *Otago Daily Times*; b. 1835,

K   Keziah (Kezzie) Wesley – youngest sibling of John and Charles; b. 1709

L   Lois Lane – girlfriend of Superman (1st comic published 1938)

Lois Muir – NZ netball, representative, coach, and administrator; b. 1935

Lydia Ko – Korean-born NZ professional golfer; b. 1997

Levi Strauss – founded first company to manufacture blue jeans; b. 1908

Linus – child with security blanket, *Peanuts* cartoon, first published 1954 (2 Timothy 4:21)

Luke Romano – All Black 2012

**M** Martha Washington – 1st USA First Lady; b. 1789

Mary Shelly – wrote *Frankenstein's Monster*, wife of poet Percy Bysshe Shelley; b. 1797

Mary Wollstonecraft – author, *A Vindication of the Rights of Women* (1792); b. 1759

Mehetabel (Hetty) Wesley – intellectually gifted sister of John Wesley; b.1697

Mehetabel Newman – Wesleyan missionary in NZ for 40 years; b. 1822

Malakai Fekitoa – All Black 2014

Mark Todd – equestrian medal winner; b. 1956

Mark Zuckerberg – co-founder of FaceBook; b. 1984

Matthew Arnold – English poet and cultural critic; b. 1822

Michael Hill – NZ jeweller; b. 1938

Michael Joseph Savage – 1st Labour PM; b. 1872

Michael King – NZ historian; b 1945

**N** Naomi Watts – British actress and film producer; b. 1968

Nathan Harris – All Black 2014

Nathaniel Turner – pioneer missionary (WMS) NZ, Tonga, Fiji; b. 1792

Noah Webster – developed the first American dictionary; b. 1843

**P** Paul McCartney – (Beatles) composer and singer; b. 1942

Paul Gauguin – French post- impressionist painter, buried in Tahiti; b. 1848

Peter Jackson – film director, screenwriter and producer; b. 1961

Peter the Great – Tsar of Russia, first Russian; b. 1672

Peter Tchaikovsky – celebrated Russian composer; b. 1840

Peter Sellars – British comedian, 'Inspector Clouseau' films; b. 1925

Peter Snell – outstanding middle distance runner, 3 Olympic gold medals; b. 1938

Philip, Duke of Edinburgh – husband of Queen Elizabeth, (born Prince Philip of Greece & Denmark); b.1921

Phillip – Admiral Arthur Phillip, first Governor of New South Wales; b. 1738

Philip Island – near Melbourne, known for its penguins

Priscilla White – real name of UK singer 'Cilla Black'; b. 1943

Priscilla Presley – wife of Elvis Presley; b. 1945

**R**   Rachel Carson – naturalist, wrote *The Silent Spring* and *The, Sea Around Us*; b. 1907

Admiral Arthur Phillip, first Governor of New South Wale; b. 1738

*Rebecca of Sunnybrook Farm* – by Kate Douglas, children's classic, published 1903

Ruth Rendell – British crime novelist; b. 1930

Reuben Thorne – All Black 1999

**S**   Sarah Palin – US politician, 9th Governor of Alaska; b. 1964

Susanna Wesley – mother of John and Charles Wesley, 'Mother of Methodism'; b. 1669

Samuel Pepys – English civil servant and diarist; b. 1631

Samuel Leigh – first Wesleyan missionary to NZ, arrived 1822; b. 1785

Samuel Marsden – first Anglican missionary to NZ, arrived 1814; b. 1765

Samuel Morse – invented Morse code; b. 1791

Seth MacFarlane – actor, singer and creator of animated TV series *Family Guy*; b. 1973

Silas – albino monk character in Dan Brown's thriller, *The Da Vinci Code*, published 2006

Silas Marner: Character in *The Weaver of Raveloe* – novel by George Elliot, published 1861

Simon Cullen – All Black 2014

Solomon Islands – Pacific islands east of Papua New Guinea

Stephen Hawking – brilliant English theoretical physicist; b. 1942

Stephen King – US horror novelist; b. 1947

**T**   Tabitha Jewellery – personalised jewellery crafted in Christchurch; established 2004

Thomas Bracken – Irish born NZ journalist and poet, wrote *God Defend New Zealand*; b. 1841

Thomas Gainsborough – English portrait painter of *The Blue Boy*; b. 1727

Timothy Spall – English character actor; b. 1957

**U**   Uriah Heep – Dicken's character; Rock band formed in London, 1969

**Z**   Zachariah Nathaniel Wood (Zac Wood) – US actor and producer; b. 1974

# Additional Resources

# Resources with a Female Focus

## Presenting Woman Story Reflections in Church

Most of the female reflections in this book can be presented in church as part of the 'sermon slot.'

The worship leader needs to either introduce or end the 'drama presentation' with a few words that tie the presentation to the theme of the service. A normal service is one hour long and a general guide for the reflection/sermon slot is not more than 20 minutes.

If the worship leader is doing the slot unaided it can be helpful to put on a headscarf, hat or tiara when in character. If the script requires a leader/narrator, it usually works best with the leader staying in the pulpit with the other readers using the lectern microphone.

Some presentations lend themselves to involving the congregation with a response, e.g.

| | |
|---|---|
| Leader: | This woman in her time and her place made a difference. This woman used initiative and courage. This woman gave others reason to be grateful. |
| **Response:** | **We give thanks for the life of (Abigail...)** |

An ending suggestion

| | |
|---|---|
| Leader: | We have heard women share their stories, |
| **Response:** | **Ordinary women living in their ordinary lives;** |
| Leader: | Only time separates them from us. |
| **Response:** | **They used initiative and courage.** |
| Leader: | By wit and will each (she) made a difference. |
| **Response:** | **By wit and will we too can make a difference.** |

## Hymn suggestions

- *Standing Before Us* – words & music by Carole Etzler © 1983
  First line: These are the women who throughout the decades…

- *A hymn to Honour Women in the Church* by Shirley Erena Murray;
  tune With One Voice 335
  First line: Come, celebrate the women who brought the church to
  birth…

- *God who sets us on a journey* – by Joy Dine; Faith Forever Singing 32,
  music Jillian Bray. Alternative tune: 'Hyfrydol' With One Voice 173

# For study groups

## Meeting Bible Women

### *A study resource – 65 Female References*

This format has various uses.  It could be used as a 15-30 minute slot of
brief encounters during an ordinary regular fellowship meeting, a rally day,
workshop session or as an on-going Bible Study – working through the
references.

### Preparation

Print selected names and references on cards. Blank visiting cards are
ideal. Use a different colour pen for the brief encounters to the in-depth
encounters. Give one card to each pair.

### Brief Encounters

In pairs, look up the reference, read and answer.

- Who was this woman?  (Name or identifier, and book.)

- What did she do?  (Facts from reference.)

- Then present in 4 sentences, as follows:

We would like to introduce _____

   She appears in the book of _____

   She was a_____

   She went (had, met, did….) _____

   - Then present in 4 sentences:

   - We would like to introduce _____.

| Introducing... | Reference |
|---|---|
| Adah | Genesis 4:17-22 |
| Keturah | Genesis 25:1-6 |
| Judith | Genesis 26:34-35; 27:46 |
| Bilhah | Genesis 30:1-5 |
| Deborah (1) | Genesis 35:8; 24:55-59 |
| Shiphrah & Puha | Exodus 1:15-21 |
| Zipporah | Exodus 2:16-20 |
| Jochebed | Exodus 6:20; 26-27 |
| Achsah | Judges 1:12-15 |
| Orpah | Ruth 1:3-5, 14-15 |
| Merab | 1 Samuel 17:23-24; 18:17-19 |
| Abishag | 1 Kings 1:1-4 |
| Jehosheba | 2 Kings 11:1-3 |
| Huldah | 2 Kings 22:14-16 |
| Zeresh | Est 5:10, 14-15; 6:12-13 |
| Job's Wife | Job 2:7-9 |
| Jemimah | Job 42:12-15 |
| King Lemuel's Mother | Proverbs 31:1-9 |
| Peter's mother-in-law | Matthew 8:14-16 |
| Herodias' daughter ('Salome') | Matthew 14:6-11 |
| Jairus' Daughter | Mark 5:22-23, 38-42; Luke 8 |
| Salome | Mark 15:40; John 19:25 |
| Anna | Luke 2:36-38 |
| Joanna | Luke 8:1-3; 24:10-11 |
| Tabitha | Acts 9:36-41 |
| Mary of Jerusalem | Acts 12:11-15 |
| Rhoda | Acts 12:12-16 |
| Lydia | Acts 16:13-15 |
| Bernice | Acts 25:13-14, 23 |
| Phoebe | Romans 16:1 |
| Lois & Eunice | 2 Timothy 1:3-5; Acts 16:1-3 |

## In-depth Encounters

- In pairs or buzz groups, read the Bible reference, round-robin style

- **Discover:** Her status and situation;

- **Feel** into her character – how do you imagine her? (age, dress, nature, bearing)

- **Discuss:** What did she do? Why did she do it? Why is this story included in the Bible? What message may there be for us in our time and place?

| Meet with… | Reference |
| --- | --- |
| Eve | Genesis 3; 4:1-2, 25; 5:3-4 |
| Hagar | Genesis 16:1-5; 21:8-20 |
| Leah | Genesis 29:16-35; 30:9-21 |
| Rachel | Genesis 31:2-33; 35:16-20 |
| Tamar (1) | Genesis 38:1-30 |
| Miriam | Exodus 15:19-20; Numbers12:1-16 |
| Mahlah | Numbers 27:1-11; 36:1-12 |
| Rahab | Josh 2:1-24; 6:22-25 |
| Deborah (2) | Judges 4:4-10; 5:1-13, 30-31 |
| Manoah's Wife | Judges 13:2-24 |
| Delilah | Judges 16:4-19 |
| Hannah | 1 Samuel 1:1-28; 2:18-21 |
| Michal | 1 Samuel 18:20-30; 19:11-18 |
| Abigail | 1 Samuel 25:2-41 |
| Endor Medium | 1 Samuel 28:3-25 |
| Bathsheba | 2 Samuel 11:2-5, 26; 12:15-24 |
| Shunammite | 2 Kings 4:8-37 |
| Tamar (2) | 2 Samuel 13:1-22 |
| Vashti | Esther 1:8-21 |
| Mary of Nazareth | Matthew 1:18-22; Luke 1: 26-56 |
| Elizabeth | Luke 1:5-25, 39-45, 56-66 |
| Herodias | Mark 6:17-29; Matthew 14:1-12 |
| Canaanite | Matthew 15:21-28; Mark 7:24-30 |
| Believer | Luke 8:40-46; Matthew 8:18-26 |
| Mary of Bethany | Luke 10:38-42; John 12:1-8 |

| Cripple | Luke 13:10-17 |
| Woman of Samaria | John 4:1-30 + 39-42 |
| Martha | John 11:17; 27 |
| Mary wife of Clopas | John 19:25; Luke 24:13-36 |
| Lydia | Acts 16:11-15 + 35-40 |
| Slave girl | Acts 16:16-24 |
| Priscilla | Acts 18:1-4 + 18-26 |

When reporting in-depth encounters to main group use the first three sentences as given for the brief encounters, then tell more of her story and your thoughts.

## Females Filed for Fun

Can you match the verbs to each woman's story?

**Old Testament:**

**God** created, **Eve** mated, **Mrs Lot** was asalted, **her daughters** bolted, **Sarah** mirthed, **Hagar** birthed, **Rebekah** kissed, **Rachel** missed, **Leah** bore, **Mrs Potiphar** swore, **Jochebed** saved, **the Princess** raved, **Miriam** danced, **Rahab** chanced, **Mahlah** requested, **her sisters** attested, **Achsah** righted, **Jael** smited, **Deborah** judged, **Delilah** grudged, **Naomi** returned, **Ruth** earned, **Orpah** went, **Merab** was sent, **Michal** loved, **Bathsheba** tubbed, **Abigail** pleaded, **Tamar** kneaded, **Abishag** warmed, **Haggith** mourned, **Hannah** prayed, **Jezebel** slayed, **Athaliah** oppressed, **Jehosheba** redressed, **Huldah** doomed, **the Shunammite** roomed, **Vashti** refused and **Esther** amused.

**New Testament:**

**Elizabeth** was amazed and **Mary** praised, **Prophet Anna** adored, **Pete's mum** was restored, **Joanna** provided, **the Canaanite** chided, **Martha** worked, **Mary** shirked, **Mrs Pilate** tried, **Salome** cried, **a servant girl** accused, **Sapphira** lied; **Dorcas** died, **Rhoda** told, **Lydia** sold, **Bernice** escorted, **Drusilla** supported; **Priscilla** talked, **Phoebe** walked, **Chloe** mentored; **Euodia** was censored; **Lois** guided; **Eunice** taught and faith was caught.

## The Book of Ruth

The Book of Ruth is ideal for a group study session as it only has only four chapters that take up no more than four pages in most bibles, and can be read aloud in 20 minutes.

Suggestions to engage deeper with the story:

1.  Read the whole story out loud involving the whole group.Photocopy and enlarge each page

    *   Highlight the spoken words giving each speaking character a different colour
    *   Speakers: Naomi, Ruth, Boaz, Kinsman, Townsfolk (everyone else)
    *   Leader: takes the role of Narrator (or delegates)

2.  Divide into 6 groups

    *   Assign a character to each (Naomi, Ruth, Boaz, Kinsman, Townsfolk)
    *   Through discussion create a personality for that character
    *   One person from each group then re-tells the story as that character

## Bible Parents and Children

Mothers and daughters in bold print

### Genesis References

| | | |
|---|---|---|
| 4:1-2 | Adam & **Eve** | Cain, Abel, Seth & other sons and daughters |
| 4:20-21 | Laban & **Adah** | Jabel, Jubal |
| 4:22 | Laban & **Zillah** | Tubal-cain, **Naamah** |
| 9:18 | Noah | Shem, Ham, Japheth |
| 11:27 | Terah | Abram/Abraham, Nahor, Haran, Sarai (20:11-12) |
| 16:15 | Abraham & **Hagar** | Ishmael |
| 21:3 | Abraham & **Sarah** | Isaac |
| 11:26-29 | Haran & **Milcah** | Lot, **Milcah, Iscah** |

| 22:20 | Nahor & **Milcah** | Uz, Buz, Kemuel, Bethuel and four more sons |
| 22:24 | Laban & **Reumah** | Tebah, Gaham, Tahash, and **Maacah** |
| 24:24-28 | Bethuel | Laban, **Rebekah** |
| 25:19-27 | Isaac & **Rebekah** | Esau, Jacob (twins) |
| 29:10 | Laban | **Leah, Rachel** and sons |
| 29-30 | Jacob & **Leah** | Reuben, Simeon, Levi, Judah, Issachar, Zebulun, **Dinah** |
| 30:5-6 | Jacob & **Bilhah** | Dan, Naphtali |
| 30:10-11 | Jacob & **Zilpah** | Gad, Asher |
| 30:25 | Jacob & **Rachel** | Joseph, Benjamin |
| 36:4 | Esau & **Adah** | Eliphaz |
| 36:4 | Esau & **Basemath** | Reuel |
| 36:4 | Esau & **Oholibamah** | Jeush, Jalam, Korah |
| 36:12 | Eliphaz & **Timna** | Amalek |
| 38 1-8 | Judah & a Canaanite* | Er, Onan, Shelah (* daughter of Shua) |
| 38 6-30 | **Tamar** & Judah | Perez, Zerah (twins) |
| 41:50-52 | Joseph & **Asenath** | Manasseh, Ephraim |
| 46:17 | Asher | Imnah, Ishvah, Ishvi, Beriah, **Serah** |

### *Other Old Testament References*

| Exodus 18:2-4 | Moses & **Zipporah** | Gershom, Eliezer |
| Exodus 6:20 | Amran & **Jochebed** | Aaron, **Miriam**, Moses |
| Numbers 26:33 | Zelophehad | **Mahlah, Hoglah, Noah, Milcah, Tirzah** |
| Joshua 1:1 | Nun | Joshua |
| Judges 13:22-24 | Manoah | Samson |
| Matthew 1:5 | Salmon & Rahab | Boaz |
| Ruth 4:13-17 | **Ruth** & Boaz | Obed |
| Job 42:14 | Job | **Jemimah, Keziah, Kerenhappuch** and sons |
| 1 Samuel 1:4 | **Peninnah** & Elkannah | Sons and daughters |

| | | |
|---|---|---|
| 1 Samuel 1:20 | **Hannah** & Elkanah | Samuel |
| 1 Samuel 14:1 | Saul & **Ahinoam** | Jonathan, **Merab, Michal** and other sons |
| 1 Chronicles 2:13-14 | Jesse | David and six other sons, **Zeruiah, Abigail** |
| 2 Samuel 3:3; 13:1 | David & **Maacah** | Absalom, **Tamar** |
| 2 Samuel 12:24 | David & **Bathsheba** | Solomon |
| 1 Samuel 1:13 | Eli | Hophni, Phinehas |
| 1 Kings 14:21 | Solomon & **Naamah** | Rehoboam |

*New Testament References*

| | | |
|---|---|---|
| Luke 1:57-60 | **Elizabeth** & Zechariah | John (the Baptist) |
| Luke 2:36 | Phanuel | **Anna** |
| Mark 6:3 | **Mary** & Joseph | Jesus, James, Joses, Judas, Simon and sisters |
| John 21:17 | Jonas / John | Simon Peter |
| Mark 1:19 & 15:40 | Zebedee & **Salome** | James, John |
| Mark 15:21 | Simon of Cyrene | Alexander, Rufus |
| 2 Timothy 1:5 & Acts 16:1 | A Greek & **Eunice** | Timothy |

## Parents of Mary the Mother of Jesus

Tradition names the parents of Mary as Anne and Joachim. They are named as such in the apocryphal Gospel of James. The Catholic Church honours them as Saints with a Feast Day and several patronages including grandparents. They are venerated by Islam as well as Christianity. The Eastern Orthodox Church uses the name Hannah, from the same root as Anna and Anne and means 'favour' or 'grace.'

### Traditional dates

- Saint Anne c. 50 BCE–12 CE; Saint Joachim c. 50 BCE–15 CE (died in Nazareth)
- Feast Day 26 July
- Patron Saints of Grandparents

According to a text from the year 145 CE, called *The Protoevangelium of James,* a man named Joachim was upset that his wife Anne was nearing the end of her child-bearing years and had not given birth.

"Joachim was exceedingly grieved, and did not come into the presence of his wife; but he retired to the desert, and there pitched his tent, and fasted forty days and forty nights, saying in himself: I will not go down either for food or for drink until the Lord my God shall look upon me, and prayer shall be my food and drink."

Similarly, Anne, "mourned in two mournings, and lamented in two lamentations, saying: I shall bewail my widowhood; I shall bewail my childlessness." Then Anne "saw a laurel, and sat under it, and prayed to the Lord, saying: O God of our fathers, bless me and hear my prayer, as You blessed the womb of Sarah, and gave her a son Isaac."

In the midst of her prayers an angel appeared and said, "The Lord has heard your prayer, and you shall conceive, and shall bring forth; and your seed shall be spoken of in all the world." At the same time an angel appeared to Joachim, saying, "Joachim, Joachim, the Lord God has heard your prayer. Go down hence; for, behold, your wife Anne shall conceive."

Then according to the story, she conceived "her months were fulfilled, and in the ninth month Anne brought forth. And she said to the midwife: What have I brought forth? And she said: A girl. And said Anne: My soul has been magnified this day. And she laid her down. And the days having been fulfilled, Anne was purified, and gave the breast to the child, and called her name Mary."

The story is seen as symbolic in that it was considered fitting for the 'Virgin Mary' to have a miraculous birth as she was thought to be sinless in all aspects, i.e. 'not tainted by original sin.'

This story echoes other Bible stories where couples were barren but is unusual in that the birth announcement concerns a girl not a boy.

The 'Solemnity of Mary's Immaculate Conception' is celebrated on 8 December, nine months before the Feast of the Birth of Mary, 8 September.

This causes some confusion with the other Christian 'immaculate conception' that of Jesus. This is celebrated on the 25 March, nine months before 25 December. The March date has connections with 'Mothering Sunday' (also called 'Mother's Day') in the UK in that it is celebrated on the 4th Sunday of Lent. A portion of Lent is always in March.

Mothering Sunday in the UK has its origins in being an annual holiday for young people employed as servants in stately homes to visit their mothers, taking gifts (sometimes cakes or articles donated by their employers) or simply bunches of flowers gathered by the wayside. Part of the tradition was attending their 'mother church' with their mothers.

# Seasonal Liturgies, Prayers and Reflections

## Advent

Advent has come
In this holy season of anticipation
Enable me to embrace Christmas in all its fullness
Help me enter the magic world of myth and story
with the unfettered imagination of a child...
Present in the moment
Living in the story

Help me meet angels in my story
May angels quell my fears
As they did for Mary and Joseph;
May angels give me safe directions
As they did for the Magi;
May angels startle me to wonder
As they did for the shepherds;
And may I be surrounded by angels...
Uplifted by the hope and peace
that evokes joy and promotes
spontaneous acts of love. Amen.

## Angels for Children

At Christmas time we see lots of decorations,
some of the nicest ones are angels.

There are many stories of Angels
Angels are God's helpers
Sometimes they are called
Messengers from God,
Sometimes Angels have wings
But sometimes they look like us.
Angels who announce good news
Are known as Herald Angels,
Angels who protect things
Are called Guardian Angels,
Some people like to think
Everyone has a Guardian Angel
Who keeps them safe.

It is a nice thing to think about
Particularly at Christmas time
Because there are lots of
Angels in the Christmas Story.

## Angel prayer for children

Dear God,
Help me meet angels in my story
May angels help me feel safe
As they did for Mary and Joseph;
May angels give me good directions
As they did for the Wise Men;
May angels surprise me with joy
As they did for the shepherds;
May I be surrounded by angels
who help me feel loved and happy;
And please show me how I can help
other people feel happy. Amen.

## Make a sparkling Angel

*Preparation:*

- Cardboard templates – draw a simple angle shape of cardboard, cut out to form a template.

- Supply of gold glitter card (bought in sheets at dollar shops) and cut to fit the template.

- Provide, pens, scissors and gold thread.

- Place the template on the non-glitter side, draw round the shape and cut it out.

- Punch a hole at the top of the head, insert thread and tie to form a loop long enough to hang on a tree. Children will need help with making the hole and tying the thread. It is best to have prepared this in advance – draw round the head, make the hole and tie the thread before giving it to children to complete.

- Children (and seniors) may like to wear them by hanging over a button or brooch.

## Christmas Intercession

Loving God we are able:
to embrace the song of the angels,
the gladness of the shepherds,
and the wisdom of the wise men.
We experience peace, hope, joy and love
because by chance we live in a land of privilege,
Our citizens expect to be treated well
in all aspects of living;
We are the products of democracy
Justice is ours of right,
Our needs are met,
Our fears are minimal,
We feast, travel and exchange presents;
Our happy land is not far away,
It is here – goodwill surrounds us.

But we know this is not how it is in many countries;
Disrespect, fear, hate, poverty and hunger blight millions.
We pause to think of those suffering at this moment…

We ask that your presence be known to them,
That those with power be moved by compassion to
do what is just and what is wise in their governance,
May ordinary people everywhere be motivated
to close doors of hate and open doors of love,
May the bars of oppressions crumble
revealing windows of opportunity.
As we remember the birth at of the Prince of Peace,
We give thanks that we personally know peace in our time.
We offer profound thanks for all the joys of Christmas
that we so casually and so easily take for granted.
Our wish is, that peace, hope, joy and love
Come to all people and all lands. Amen.

## Prayer of Intercession

God, we confess we are prone to forgetting
what we are and what we should be.
There are times when we are overcome by needs,
personal desires saturate our thinking and being.

Forgive us lapses of perception, forgive us
for putting ourselves at the centre of your universe,
and for looking to you as a magician in our service.
Remind us, if this were so you would be less than us.
Forgive, O God all our errant presumptions.

May we never forget that you are the Almighty One,
You are Divine Mystery, the Power, the Glory
and the Energy of the universe.
You are the One who defined the limits of the earth
and furnished it with life teeming in diversity.
You are the God who speaks from whirlwinds
and you are the still small voice within.

Keep us ever mindful of our smallness,
yet confident that we are loved and have value.
As harvest grain is greater than tall standing stalks
may we understand the importance of smallness.

We give thanks to you for igniting within us the divine spark of
compassion, and gifting us language, reflection and creativity.
We know we are not mere creatures bound by instinct,
We know we are individuals, each unique and special,
We know, because we have the ability to give and receive love.

Our growth is from independence to interdependence,
Help us understand how life in fullness is not independence.
May our perspective not be 'suffering from' but 'suffering with.'
Remind us that we do not have to carry our burdens alone.
In silence we now bring to you, the names of those we care about…
Amen.

## Journeys

The journey motif is universal in its appeal. Ancient myths from all parts of the world embrace the theme of a journey. As do modern myths from Dorothy in Oz, to Tom Sawyer, Luke Skywalker and Harry Potter. Journeys involve stepping out into the unknown, excitement is in the air, adventure awaits, and with adventure, there is always risk. People return from a journey knowing more than they knew before, enriched by new facts, new encounters and new spiritual awareness.

Many Bible heroes embark on a journey – significant Hebrew males being Abraham, Moses and Jacob. Among women is Rebecca who set out by camel to marry a cousin she had never met, also Zipporah, Achsah and Abigail who travelled by donkey and interceded on behalf of their husbands. Better known are Naomi and Ruth who travelled on foot. For Naomi the journey was bitter, her redemption came after she returned home. For Ruth the journey was one of anticipation and fulfilment.

## A Blessing for the Journey

Every life is a journey,
Every life needs a blessing,
Every path offers dangers and delights,
Every aspect can be enhanced
by the knowledge we are not alone.

We ask your blessing on the moves we make.
At our beginnings we have no choices,
We are reliant on love for our nurture.
As horizons widen and choices present
May we not forget love is what nurtures.

Bless us at every turn, guide our choices,
Prompt us to delight in the joys of the journey,
Encourage us to live fully,
To give generously,
To love well,
and to reach home knowing we are loved.

## Easter Leaves

In
the cathedral of the park
autumn trees stand tall and stark
leaves in crimson gold and browns
are transformed by Easter gowns
dancing flakes of fractured light
delight in brief unfettered flight
reflect deflect and genuflect
as they bound and mound
making stained-glass
patterns on the
ground

April
leaves
are tumbling
down the driveway
with rustle and flutter
holding meetings in the
yard where they leap
heap and mutter
then they skitter
down the street
to carpet the
gutter

In
autumn leaves
wear golden brown
or gowns of russet red
free at last to see the town
they hustle bustle down
where they keep on
dancing prancing
even though
they are
dead

Yes
yes
the
summer dies
and winds roam leaden skies
the once green leaves are dead
earth-bound now in heaps of red
all are fading some quite brown
fibre crumbles and seeps down
composting to enrich the earth
from dark humus comes rebirth
new seeds germinate and grow
nurtured well from soil below
death and life together bind
forming strange connection
when touched by God we
also find surprising
resurrection

## Palms for Holy Week

"Hosanna"
cry the fickle
crowd as Jesus
Christ rides by
You are the one
Go! get it done!
We want a King
Go do your thing
Hurray! Bravo!
Go Jesus go
go
go
go
go
go

"Crucify"
cry the fickle
crowd, as Jesus
stumbles by,
You're not the one
Be gone be done!
This useless thing
Is not Our King
Not Our Christ
No Jesus no
no
no
no
no
no
no

"It is
finished"
Jesus cried
To this crowd
the King is dead
Yet He's not gone
Our Lord lives on
Present in slums
present in steeple
and present in us
The Easter People.
Christ lives today
in all who say,
Yes God yes
yes
yes
yes
yes
yes
yes

## Prayer for Mothers and Others

Love-maker, Pain-bearer, Mother and Father of us all,
We know that no matter what we do your love is unconditional,
Help us to justify your love by living loving lives.

On this Home and Family Sunday we give special thanks for families.
From our earliest days we had relations to call our own,
We thank you that we were born into a family.

Bless all families – nuclear families, single-parent families,
separated families,
inter-generational families, blended families, chosen families,
foster families…
Whatever its composition, may each family be a unit of love.

We pray also for the extended family – grandparents, uncles, aunts,
nephews, nieces, cousins, step-children and God-children.
Enable each to play their part and know the joy of connectedness.

Bless all adults who interact with children and young people.
May they enjoy this responsibility
and mentor with wisdom and patience.
Equip and re-equip each of us for our ever-changing society.

We give thanks for fathers and the particular parenting they bring.
We give thanks for mothers and the particular parenting they bring.
Help all parents fulfil their roles with competency and joy.

As our country celebrates Mothers' Day
we give special thanks for mothers.
Thank you for creating the concept of motherhood
and the gift of mothering.
Enable all motherly women to put their mothering skills
to good purpose.

Help us to carry and share the best things we learned from our mothers.
In silence we name our mothers and their virtues before you…
We think of our own mothers and offer our thanks.

Bless each mother represented here, wherever she may be.
Bless us, the children of mothers, and the children of you,
May we be worthy of the relationship. Amen.

# Queen's Birthday

*A fitting time to reflect on Queens in Scripture*

We citizens of the Commonwealth are blessed with a Christian queen who takes her civic and religious duties seriously. All round the world Anglican congregations pray for her every Sunday.

Various Queens are named in Scripture, but few are given stories. (The term 'king' appears over 2,000 times, 'queen' around 50.) A Hebrew king could have many wives but who he was related to was his heritage, thus Queen Mothers were given special status in Hebrew courts.

King Lemuel's mother is often overlooked as readers rush to extol the virtues of the impossibly good wife that follows her advice in the last chapter of Proverbs. Be cheered to know that final section is in reality an acrostic poem, each verse beginning with a different letter of the Hebrew alphabet, devised as a teaching aid for young men as a guide in what to look for in a wife. It is not simply a list of domestic skills, business skills such as buying fields are also prized.

Who King Lemuel ruled over we do not know but as his name contains 'el' another name for Yahweh. God must have been important to him. In ancient times, as now, Mothers were the first teachers of their young. It is reassuring that this adult king remembered lessons learned at his mother's knee, and as an adult wanted to give her the credit, placing her wisdom above that of his courtly advisors. The motherly advice she instilled rates with the best in the book – advice suitable for ancient kings and modern Christians...

### Proverbs 31:1-9, NRSV

### The Teaching of King Lemuel's Mother

[1] The words of King Lemuel. An oracle that his mother taught him: [2] No, my son! No, son of my womb! No, son of my vows! [3] Do not give your strength to women, your ways to those who destroy kings. [4] It is not for kings, O Lemuel, it is not for kings to drink wine, or for rulers to desire strong drink; [5] or else they will drink and forget what has been decreed, and will pervert the rights of all the afflicted. [6] Give strong drink to one who is perishing, and wine to those in bitter distress; [7] let them drink and forget their poverty, and remember their misery no more. [8] Speak out for those who cannot speak, for the rights of all the destitute. [9] Speak out, judge righteously, defend the rights of the poor and needy.

Colin Gibson has taken some of these words and put them into a song for justice: No. 126 in *Hope Is Our Song*. First line: Speaking up for those who cannot speak…

## An Acrostic Psalm

(Inspired by Psalm 111, an acrostic psalm in Hebrew)

Awake to your potential
Be filled with the Holy spirit;
Come soul mates in the Lord
Delight in goodness,
Embrace the abundance
Found all around, for
God's goodness is here,
Here in this small place and
In the vastness of all Creation.
Joy is ours, for
Kindness surrounds and
Love abounds.
May we live as God's kin,
Never forgetting the
One who showed us how.
Pray with your heart,
Quiet your mind,
Reflect on Christ,
Stay strong in love,
Trust in truth,
Understand imperfection,
Validate life, seek
Wisdom from within, and
'Xpand your soul to let the
Yeast of God's goodness bring
Zest to those you encounter.

# A Winter's Day Retreat

## Alone with God, I sit in solitude

**I feel**
crisp air
   sun patches, and chill threads

**I smell**
the sharpness of winter
   fresh as an iced drink
      with a waft of exhaust

**I see**
entwined branches
   curving upward
      twigs fanning
         the blue, blue, sky
  In shifted gaze
a church tower stands solid against the sun's low glare

**I hear**
birds chirp urgent gossip
   spasmodic engine roar
      the zoom of distant jet
         a jogger pound past
            water gurgle in a sump
               the voice of a child

      **Alone with God I sit tending my own needs**
      A child trots past chatting uphill
      to the father hand that holds hers.
        In their wake a woman pushes an empty buggy.
      "Mummm," floats the wail of a straggling toddler.
    "No, nooo, no!" the small voice snaps silent.
  The child freezes as I fill its gaze.
  The mother calls back down the path.
  Her charge veers onto the grass
  demanding my attention
    with unblinking concentration.
      'Come,' urges the mother
        The tot is unmoved.
        Unbidden the sister patters back

running down the sloping path,
'I'll carry you,' she pipes.
Wrapping small arms round the other she
lifts him two inches clear of the ground.

**I sense**

The paradox of city life...
  trees and traffic
  sun and sump
  chill and church
  solitude and interaction
birds and babes in arms
and God in all.

## A Prayer of Approach for Bible Sunday

Spirit of Life
As we struggle to understand your Holy Word
Open our minds to exciting possibilities
Free us to respond to the power of story;
Teach us, delight us, and move us on,
For your song is true,
Your voice is love,
May your holy words power us to holy thinking
and open us to engaging with you. Amen.

## A Prayer of Determination

God, as citizens of Aotearoa we come to you in shock.
Unprecedented slaughter has taken place in our land.

Though aware your wonderful world
has been marred by human violence
since humans learnt to fear each other,
people of faith experience the Divine,
by whatever name, as a god of loving kindness.
We know you are with all victims,
loving them as parents love their children,
comforting and supporting,
and blessing those who care for them ...
We add our love to yours.

As a Christian community we believe
you sowed in humankind the seeds of love
and sent the Christ to teach us how
to increase the yield of compassion.
As global understanding grew
replacing fear 'of other' with wisdom,
we expected ignorance to diminish.
We believe the vast majority of humans embrace
goodness and kindness as the essence of being human,
yet, pockets of distrust and evil persist ...

But, not in New Zealand!
Mass murder has remained outside our experience.
Now we have discovered we are not immune,
hate crime respects no boundaries.
For all our lofty and smug ideals
we are citizens of a world infested with terror.

New Zealand was selected to prove nowhere is safe.
This evil was deliberately inflicted on Christchurch,
a city rebuilding lives and structures,
bravely recovering from our biggest
natural disaster in recent times.

Filled with disgust by this targeted atrocity,
We stand with our Prime Minister asserting,
"Terrorists have no place in our country
... we utterly reject them."
We support our Muslim sisters and brothers
and all who want to live in peace.

In this unprecedented situation
We Kiwis will cling to love.
So help us God. Amen.

## April (2019)

Today we meet mindful of the futility of war...
The suffering, pain and destruction it inflicts;
The waste and trauma, and long shadows
war casts down generations.

We pray that all humankind
will evolve beyond this
primitive concept of
violence being a solution.

Despite our physical distance from
the current atrocities of war
we hold war memories –
personal or passed down to us.
We pray for family members
whose lives were terminated
or blighted by war...

Much to our shock, horror and shame
we who at the bottom of the map
can no longer claim
physical distance from terrorism...
hideous actions delivered under tags of
rights, retribution, justice and entitlement.

Graphic images that reach our screens
delivered by ever-present 'breaking news'
camera angles are no longer
merely 'News of the World.'
We have seen images of our streets
and our people delivered of by
our cameras, TV 1 and TV 3
and phone videos taken by Kiwis.

Whatever the cause may be
we pray for all who suffer;
We think of them with love
asking that our love
be added to your goodness
in the efforts of bring healing
to all who are harmed.

We pray for those in power
who treat others as pawns;
And those who feel powerless
and see killing as their right.
May such persons know what they do
and be motivated to cease from evil
and find solutions in compassion,
mutual respect, and true liberty for all. Amen.

## General intercession

We meet as people of privilege
Who live in a pleasant land
Where kindness and care
is our expectation.

We offer profound thanks
Keep us mindful
Of the many places
and millions of people, unable
to live with these expectations
due to oppression and greed
the lack of will and resources.

We pray for the people
who suffer in these places
and those who could help.
Show us how we can best help
alleviate suffering wherever
we encounter it.

Even where kindness and care
are the seen as the standard norm
people are mistreated, and often
it goes unnoticed, or is ignored.
If we have been part of this
we ask your forgiveness.

Help us to be more aware
and vigilant in speaking out
and taking positive action.

We pray for those in our country
who suffer due to their appearance,
age, gender, or social status,
lack of possessions or lack of skills.
Give those who suffer the strength
to keep believing in goodness;
And those who inflict suffering
the will to show goodness.

We pray for all who suffer discrimination
because they are seen as different,
due to: ethnicity, religion, sexual orientation,
mental impairment or physical impairment.
Give them the strength to believe
they are people of worth;
And may people everywhere learn to
to replace fear with understanding
and apathy with empathy. Amen.

## House Blessing Ritual

Grace and peace be with you. We gather to celebrate this home and to ask God's blessing on this house and on those who dwell therein. This house has been occupied by others. We do not know what joys and sorrows this house has seen. What has happened has happened. The past has passed.

Now this family _____ (name each member) claim this space as their special place.

A new era has begun for this house and for those who dwell here.

### A Candle Ritual

**1st child**

Some experiences were good
Some experiences were not good
We are all shaped by our past.

As the eldest child of this family
I have the longest past.
I light this candle for the past. (Light candle)

**2nd child**

Some experiences are good
Some experiences are not good

As the middle child of this family
I live surrounded by family.
I take good light from the past
to light this candle for the present. (Light candle)

**3rd child**

Some experiences will be good
Some experiences will not be good

As the youngest child in this family
I live in the present.
From the good light of the present
I light this candle for the future. (Light candle)

**All together**

Light overcomes dark;
We live in the light of the present
shaped by the light of the past
looking forward to the light to come. Amen.

*Concluding Blessings*

Loving God whatever the future brings, give those who live here
enough strength to cope, and enough love to share. Surround this house
and household with your love, this day, this night and every day and
every night. Amen.

## A Liturgy for All, Regardless of Label

*Call to worship*

To the God who walks on wounded feet and heals with wounded hands,
To the God who stands beside us wounded, all knowing and all loving,
To the God of imperfections
We offer our imperfect praise,
Trusting in the perfect love of the God
who knows what it is to be truly human.

*Prayer of approach*

God of pain and God of peace, Mother and Father of us all,
Created in your image we inherited what makes us human,
The ability to think, communicate, reflect, record and create.
These gifts are precious, and we give you thanks.

Though we have gifts in common, we are not all alike,
Each of us is a different individual, unique and special,
We come before you rejoicing in difference.

We come before you knowing each child is given a different blend
of gifts and experiences, that shape, and keep shaping the adult.

Every person in your world is differently abled,
Every person in your world is differently disabled
Help each of use what we can to enhance our lives and your world.
Amen.

### Offering

God, help us to know the truth of your love in our lives;
Enable us to grow in the grace we need
to be agents of change for a better world.
We dedicate ourselves and our gifts to your service. Amen.

### Prayer of intercession

God of our yesterdays
and God of our tomorrows
we ask that you be with us now,
God of our today.

We are an Easter People!
We have experienced the resurrection,

Yet often we behave like your pre-Easter followers,
uncertain and unprepared.
Help us claim our Easter heritage
and live with confidence.

Equip us for what is to come.
Help us to travel light
carrying what is best from the past to the future.

God of Vision and New Possibilities
open our hearts and minds to the reality of your presence.
God of Light illuminate the dark places of our lives.
We are not perfect people.
Come through the cracks of our imperfections
and fill us with your light.

We pray for all marginalised people.
Those who suffer discrimination because of gender, race,
sexual orientation, physical or mental impairment.
Give them strength and belief in their worth.

We pray for those active in discrimination,
and those who allow it to happen.
May they know what they do.
May they understand the hurts they cause.

We gather our thoughts in this sacred place
knowing that you have heard each sincere desire.
We long for a time when all people are valued.

May our unconditional love flow from us to others
May it swirl and curl through this year
embracing all who seek a better life. Amen.

**Hymn** *Alleluia Aotearoa* 158: Who is my mother, who is my brother…
(Murray/Render)

### Affirmation

With your help O God:
We reject victim mentality – we will live as survivors
We will do the best we can - we will be people of faith.

For the God who walks on wounded feet
and heals with wounded hands,
For the God who stands beside us wounded, all knowing and all loving,
For the God of imperfections,
We go into our wonderful and imperfect world
to reflect God's perfect love,
and in so doing, claim what it is to be truly human.

*Disability Sunday in NZ – 3rd Sunday in June*
*UN International Day of Persons with Disabilities 3 December*

God who creates light from darkness
We come before you with eyes closed and minds open,
We bring dark queries from the depths of our souls,
and ask for your continuing illumination.

May our glimmerings gather increasing brightness
but save us from the false security of finite knowledge.

May we never cease to question, ponder and wonder,
Keep our souls alert and active.

We name our sorrows before you…
Bless our sorrows with the warmth of empathy.

We name our fears before you…
Help our fears lessen in the light of your love.

Be a light to our path and the paths of all who seek goodness.
Bring light to darkness of the world. Amen.

*A Commission*

Go rejoicing in difference,
We go to love.
Go open to diversity,
We go to hear.
Go willing to cope with division,
We go to care.

## Reflecting on Stories and Aging

As the old hymn says God has given us a book full of stories. The trouble is we often forget the Bible is composed of stories – ancient stories, folk-stories, poetry and ponderings, as humans from bygone eras sought to understand what a worthy God may require of them.

In Creation only humans, with their unique gift of language, are able to tell and record stories. All cultures live stories and create stories. The role of story is to entertain, inform and inspire. In the world of story, it is irrelevant to ask, did this really happen? The important question to ask of any story is what is the message?

The answer can be different things to different people, and different times evoke different thoughts. To reach in-depth answers requires delving beneath the surface looking into when it was written, why it was written, and for whom it was written. Then the in-depth reader/listener is better equipped to ask what could the message of this story be for me in my situation?

When considering Elizabeth, for me, the message is not that she had a baby late in life. I see Elizabeth as an example of how to live as an older woman. Like Anna she is a good woman, religious and intuitive. Elizabeth is also modest, caring and hospitable. She was not looking for extra blessings. She was content with what she had.

It is oft quoted the happiest people are not those who have the most but those who make the most of what they have. Wherever we live our landscape becomes part of us. In New Zealand we are particularly blessed by landscape, every person lives near a physical feature of spiritual significance. The longer we live in a beautiful landscape the more we become part of it. The trick of aging well is to appreciate what we have. 'Kapiti Islands' are everywhere.

Give us, we pray, the wisdom to value the concept of teamwork,
And the grace to recognise the pitfalls of separateness;
May we grow beyond independence to interdependence.
Help us develop good partnerships in love, in life, in leisure,
May mutual respect be the foundation of all our relationships.
Give us the wisdom to know when to speak
and when to refrain from speaking;
Enable us to listen carefully, and hear with sensitivity,
And in so doing, bring true understanding of Jesus
into our moment of history. Amen.

For the myriad of unremarkable women:
Struggling women, suffering women, and ourselves we pray…
Strengthen our sisterhood as together we work for a better world;
Show us how to become more like the woman we admire.
**God bless ordinary women.**

Enable us to claim the best in feminist values and feminine wisdom;
Help us reveal the Spiritual within the Material,
and the Sacred within the Secular.
With strong threads from the past
and rays of bright hope for the future,
Help us weave a faith suitable for today –
a mantle worthy of tomorrow's daughters.
**God bless us all. Amen.**

### Kapiti Island – A Prayer for Simple Pleasures

God, let me never be too careworn not to giggle
to wriggle my toes and tickle my soul.

May I not be too overwrought,
or grounded in responsibility
to notice the blue of the sky
and to see fluffy hippopotami
puffing after billowing white snails.

May I never be too tired to kick off my shoes
and squeal as the sea ices my toes with wet foam.

May my eyes ever delight in the bush clad shapes
that rise as hills to the east and an island to the west.

May Kapiti Island always rise on my horizons
majestic as a galleon under full sail
a splendid spectacle rigged for adventure.

May I soar in imagination as a gull
catch the updrafts and glide free
unfettered by care, over the sparkling sea
over Kapiti's zig-zagging peaks
towards the golden deep that holds the sinking sun.

And back again to my life because
there are mysteries I do not need to explore
It is enough to catch the vision of life gilded
to know unexpected joys are everywhere. Amen.

### Prayer of Approach

Immortal God, in you we trust;
we give thanks for the eternal assurance of faith.
We come from a long tradition of those who seek you
in the community of Church.
We meet now in this place seeking to enrich our faith through worship.
We seek release from all that would hinder us from encountering you.

Invisible God, in you we trust; we give thanks for the intangibles
that confirm your reality to those who believe:
the comfort of love; the ability to trust;
the hope that faith keeps resurrecting,
Enable us to use our faith to do justice and love kindness.

Wise God, in you we trust;
we give thanks that you are there when we understand,
and you are there when we don't understand.
We come in faith. We come seeking to be better people
Grant us the wisdom to walk in humble confidence with you.

God of justice, kindness and mercy,
May we never forget we are made in your image;
Help us nurture the goodness you seeded in humankind,
Grant us a vibrant faith that increasingly reflects more of you.
As we live within you, may you live within us. Amen.

Surprising God,
**You meet us in ways we do not expect.**
We ask for success:
**You teach us acceptance.**
We ask to be loved:
**You ask us to love**
We ask for ease
**You challenge us.**
We ask for certainty:
**You fill us with questions.**
We expect to find you in piety:
**And discover you can be found anywhere.**
We expect you to use the best people:
**Yet you often use the most unlikely folk\**
We are glad of this God
**Because our hope is that you will use us. Amen.**

## Offertory for Spring

Renewing God
As we contemplate the season of spring
we see connection between coins and seeds;
Both come in various sizes and colours,
and bear different markings,
are symmetrical and fit in pockets.
Held in our gaze they appear lifeless
yet both hold the power of transformation.

We ask that you bless our coins
and paper dollars, brought here today
unseen cheques and bank transfers.
May our offerings be placed in
environments that permit them to fulfil
their potential of bringing beauty and health
to this world we all share. Amen.

## Commission

Go in hope – assured of a God who understands
what it means to be human
Go in faith – announce a God who never tires in love for humankind,
Go inspired – for this is the Good News for all humanity.

## Song: Let there be peace on earth

1. Let there be peace on earth
   And let it begin with me:
   Let there be peace on earth,
   The peace that was meant to be.
   With God always with us
   Family all are we.
   Let us walk together
   In perfect harmony.

2. Let peace begin with me,
   Let this be the moment now.
   With every step I take,
   Let this be my solemn vow:
   To take each moment
   and live each moment
   In peace eternally.
   Let there be peace on earth
   and let it begin with me.

*Words & Music: Sy Miller, Jill Jackson*
*Adapted by Philip Garside (2018)*

## Where is Wisdom?

The Proverbs suggest:
Tho' Lady Wisdom can be found,
Dame Folly sits on every mound,
Calling, cajoling, laughing loud,
Her relish is to sway the crowd.

Lady Wisdom dwells in the light,
Admitting those who crave insight;
Her honest table does sustain,
Mature thought her guests attain.

Dame Folly gives an easy fix,
But with them both we all will mix.
It is our choice to do what's right,
It's not set down in black and white;
To make the Scriptures live for now
We must wrestle with why and how.

*Proverbs 9*

## Our Holy Book

We give thanks for your written word, our Bible,
a rare and sacred gift, yet so readily available to us.
The Holy Bible has inspired and guided through the ages.
For us it is a revered book of poetry, prose and problems,
An ancient story book filled with diverse stories of people of old
Beginning with a tale of a garden and ending with a city of gold.
In its pages we encounter the struggle of an ancient people
searching for a worthy God, and what that God requires of them.
They don't always get it right, but neither do we in our time.
Help us delve carefully into its sacred myths and mysteries,
Grant us deepening understanding of its legends and laws,
Help us to delight in knowing and recalling its sacred wisdom
So we can best apply its Good News to our lives in our times. Amen.

## A Seed is a Promise

Suitable for Springtime, Harvest Festival, or New Year

Pass bowls of mixed seeds around the congregation and invite everyone to take one seed and examine it carefully (sunflower, pumpkin, beans, pips etc).

### Call to worship

| | |
|---|---|
| Leader: | Welcome to the garden of our church community. |
| **All:** | **We come bearing the seeds of promise.** |
| Leader: | Seeds need to be planted and nurtured. |
| **All:** | **We will grow in our unique ways in this place and we will be nurtured by our Creator.** |
| Leader: | Do we know what our garden will become? |
| **All:** | **No, we do not know the future of our group.** |
| Leader: | But we will continue in faith and hope. |
| **All:** | **We will strive to fulfill our potential.** |

### Discuss with the person next to you:

- Can you identify your seed? (guess if you can't.)
- Describe what your seed could become?
- Share an experience of planting a seed
- Share an experience of picking flowers
- Share an experience of picking fruit or berries

*Contribute*

- Call out (brain-storm) words that could be used to describe gardens

*Concluding words*

Create a mind picture of a beautiful garden … take a closer look at your little seed … imagine planting it in that garden. Where would you put it? How would you prepare the soil?

Every seed carries a promise. If given the right conditions, it will grow. Once upon a time God planted a garden. Our oldest tales tell of human-kind experiencing God in a garden. God walked and talked with the first humans in the context of a garden. That garden represented perfection. A garden is a place to be enjoyed but it is also a place of labour. The best gardens are formed by God and humankind working together. Humans bring their ideas and labour, but without God's blessing of life and growth, there is no yield.

*Prayer*

Creator God we ask for your blessing. We often feel insignificant, but we are people of promise. You seeded each of us with divine potential. Help us nurture ourselves and each other so we may grow to be the creative, thoughtful people that you intended us to be. Amen.

## Prayer: Breath of the Spirit

Breath of the Spirit come blow among us
fill and inspire us, with life-giving joy.

Weave your deft patterns, reform and reshape us
link us together to form a new whole.

Roar down our streets – winter gale blowing
sweep clean our dark places – hearts bare and renewed

Uplift and free us, help us to soar
May your energy power us, turn all hearts to you.

Breath of the Spirit come blow among us|
fill and inspire us, with life-giving joy.

*Philip Garside, 2016*
*Song and litany settings here:*
https://tinyurl.com/y3zju4yu

# Eve

(Selected verses)

Adam stood by a sleeping lion
Feeling its fur with his toes,
He did not hear Eve approaching,
Like a shy fawn she crept close.

Anyway, what could he do?
She'd already eaten it first.
She could not have all the wisdom
He'd have to eat and be cursed.

This was no Fall, but Creation,
For although the Terrible Voice
Condemned them to sweat and to labour,
They had conquered the power of choice.

As the Flaming Sword receded
Eve walked a little ahead.
"If we keep on using this knowledge
I think we'll be back," she said.

*F R Scott*

Eve ventured into the unknown and reached back to bring Adam with her to a new world of mortal demands and moral decisions. Myth is at the spiritual heart of all cultures. Myth is not stories told by primitives. Myth is truth told by geniuses. The Eden Story is a mythical description of humankind leaving the world of animal existence and entering the problematic world of being human. How we view Eve colours our view of ourselves, and our view of others. Created in God's image we have the sacred responsibility to be creative. Meaning is held in story. Our experiences are our story. We need myths for our time. For the Christian myth is developed in the light of Christ. This light calls us to value every person and the story that makes them who they are. We are part of God's continuing story...

## Closing Blessing

Blessings abound, accept the bounty;
Be invigorated by the Holy Spirit,
Be empowered by Scripture and story;
Know God speaks through Scripture,
Know God speaks through story,
Know God is in your story,
Know God speaks through you.
Amen.

# References & Acknowledgements

- *Biblical Affirmations of Woman,* Leonard Swidler, Westminster John Knox Press 1979

- *Do What You Have the Power to Do,* Helen Bruch Pearson, Upper Rooms Books, Nashville 1992

- *Women's Bible Commentary,* Carol A. Newson & Sharon H. Ringe, Westminster John Knox Press 1998

- *Judges and Method,* Gale A. Yee, Fortress Press, Minneapolis, 1999

- With sincere thanks to Revs Judith McKinlay and Nan Burgess (Knox College/Otago University Dunedin, New Zealand) for their inspirational teaching.

# Index of Women Named in this Book

**A**

Abi 136, 138
Abigail 11, 22, 79, 85, 136, 137, 140, 141, 153, 154, 157, 164
Abihail 136
Abijah 136, 138
Abijam 136, 138
Abishag 83, 86, 87, 140, 141, 152, 154
Abital 136, 137
Achsah 37, 49, 53, 141, 152, 154, 164
Adah 141, 152, 155, 156
Adams, Abigail 144
Ahinoam 85, 136, 137, 157
Ana 143
Anahera 143
Angel 143
Ani 143
Anna 88, 103, 104, 105, 141, 143, 144, 152, 154, 157, 158, 179
Anne 158
Annesley, Elizabeth 120, 121
Annesley, Mary (White) 120
Ann Turner 132
An Unknown Wife 11
Apphia 141
Argula von Grumbach 114, 117, 118
Aroha 143
Asenath 78, 141, 156
Athaliah 136, 137, 138, 139, 141, 154
Azuba 136, 138

**B**

Basemath 136, 138, 141, 156
Bathsheba 37, 59, 83, 85, 136, 137, 141, 153, 154, 157
Bernice 140, 141, 143, 152, 154
Berry, Ursula 123
Betsy, servant girl 133

Bilhah 141, 152, 156
Bithiah 140, 141
Button, Lenna 114, 127, 130

**C**

Cain's wife 77
Canaanite Woman 37, 69, 153
Candace 140, 141
Carson, Rachel 148
Chloe 141, 144, 154
Claudia 141, 143
Cozbi 141

**D**

Damaris 141
Deborah 37, 51, 54, 141, 143, 152, 153, 154
Delilah 53, 141, 153, 154
Dinah 75, 76, 78, 79, 141, 156
Dorcas 141, 143, 144, 154
Drusilla 141, 143, 154

**E**

Eglah 136, 137
Ehetere 143
Elisheba 141
Elizabeth 88, 103, 105, 141, 143, 153, 154, 157, 179
Elizabeth II 145
Endor, Medium at 37, 57, 58, 153
Erihapeti 143
Esther 11, 25, 26, 28, 67, 68, 140, 141, 143, 153, 154
Eunice 11, 34, 141, 143, 152, 157
Euodia 141, 154
Eve 37, 38, 39, 40, 76, 77, 141, 143, 153, 154, 155, 186

**F**

Fairburn, Sarah 133

**G**

Gomer 141
Gunn, Elizabeth 128

**H**

Hadassah 25, 136
Hagar 14, 88, 89, 90, 91, 92, 93, 100,
    141, 153, 154, 155
Haggith 60, 83, 136, 137, 141, 154
Hamutal 136, 139
Hana 143
Hannah 11, 19, 20, 103, 104, 141,
    143, 153, 154, 157, 158
Hephzibah 136, 138, 141
Hera 143
Herodias 140, 141, 152, 153
Hoglah 17, 18, 136, 141, 156
Hohipine 143
Hūhana 143
Huldah 137, 141, 152, 154
Hūria 143
Hutita 143

**I**

Iscah 141, 155
Iuriti 143
Iwa 143

**J**

Jael 52, 53, 141, 154
Jairus' Daughter 152
Jarvis, Anna 144
Jecholiah 136, 138
Jedidah 60, 136, 139
Jehoaddan 136, 138
Jehosheba 137, 140, 152, 154
Jemimah 141, 152, 156
Jephthah's Daughter 88, 99
Jephthah's Wife 98
Jerusha 136, 138
Jezebel 37, 62, 63, 136, 138, 139,
    141, 154
Joanna 88, 110, 141, 152, 154
Job's Wife 152

Jochebed 15, 141, 152, 154, 156
Judith 40, 141, 143, 152, 188
Julia 141, 143
Junias 141

**K**

Karauria 143
Keren-happuch 141, 156
Kerr, Deborah 144
Keturah 141, 152
Keziah 141, 156
King Lemuel's Mother 152, 168
Ko, Lydia 146
Kubler-Ross, Elizabeth 145

**L**

Lawry, Hephzibah 145
Leah 88, 94, 130, 141, 143, 153, 154,
    156
Lilith 141
Little Hebrew Maid 88, 101, 102
Lois 34, 141, 143, 152, 154
Lot, Mrs 154
Lumley, Joanna 145
Lydia 88, 112, 141, 143, 152, 154

**M**

Maacah 136, 137, 138, 139, 140, 141,
    156, 157
Maata 143
Mahlah 11, 17, 18, 141, 153, 154,
    156, 193
Manoah, Wife of 37, 53, 54, 153
Mara 80, 81
Martha 37, 73, 74, 141, 143, 154
Mary Magdalene 73, 110
Mary - Mother of Jesus 56, 73, 82,
    103, 104, 105, 141, 143, 153,
    154, 157, 158, 159, 160, 161
Mary of Bethany 73, 153, 154
Mary of Jerusalem 152
Mary wife of Clopas 154
McKinlay, Judith 40
Medlicott, Judith 145

Mehetabel 140, 141
Merab 83, 84, 85, 86, 87, 140, 141,
    152, 154, 157
Mere 143
Meri 143
Meshullemeth 136, 138
Michal 60, 75, 83, 84, 86, 87, 136,
    137, 140, 141, 153, 154, 157
Milcah 18, 41, 155, 156
Miriam 11, 15, 54, 141, 143, 153,
    154, 156
Miriama 143
Moses, Anna Mary Robertson 144
Muir, Lois 146

**N**

Naamah 136, 138, 141, 155, 157
Nain, Widow of 141
Naomi 37, 75, 80, 141, 154, 155, 164
Nehushta 136, 139, 141
Newman, Mehetabel 147
Noadiah 141
Noah 17, 18, 141, 155, 156
Nympha 141

**O**

Oholibamah 156
Olympas 141
Orange, Claudia 144
Orpah 141, 152, 154
Orphah 80

**P**

Palin, Sarah 148
Paquin, Anna 144
Peninnah 19, 20, 141, 156
Pereniki 143
Persis 141
Petani 143
Peter's mother-in-law 152
Pharaoh's daughter 15, 140
Phoebe 141, 152, 154
Pipi 143
Pirihira 143
Pōrina 143

Potiphar, Mrs 154
Presley, Priscilla 147
Prisca 141
Priscilla 11, 32, 141, 143, 154
Puah 141
Puddle-Duck, Jemima 145

**Q**

Queen of Sheba 140, 141

**R**

Rachel 54, 77, 94, 95, 96, 103, 141,
    143, 153, 154, 156
Rahab 37, 43, 44, 45, 46, 47, 48, 81,
    82, 141, 153, 154, 156
Rāhera 143
Raiana 143
Rea 143
Rebecca 143, 164
Rebekah 37, 41, 42, 51, 77, 141, 154,
    156
Rendell, Ruth 148
Reumah 141, 156
Reynolds, Elva 194
Rhoda 141, 152, 154
Rīpeka 143
Riria 143
Rizpah 137, 141
Roberts, Julia 145
Roihi 143
Roka 143
Ruruhira 143
Rūta 143
Ruth 48, 80, 81, 82, 112, 141, 143,
    152, 154, 155, 156, 164

**S**

Salome 141, 152, 154, 157
Samaria, Woman of 154
Samson's mother 103
Sapphira 141, 154
Sarah 11, 13, 42, 54, 77, 91, 103,
    141, 143, 154, 155, 158
Sarai 13, 89, 90, 91, 92, 141, 155
Serah 141, 156

Sheerah 141
Shelly, Mary 147
Shiphrah 141, 152
Shriver, Eunice Kennedy 145
Shunammite 153, 154
Slave girl 154
Sophia 2, 11, 12
Syntyche 141

**T**

Tabitha 141, 143, 152
Tahpenes 140, 141
Tamar 75, 76, 78, 79, 85, 87, 140,
    141, 153, 154, 156, 157
Taphath 136, 138, 141
Tapita 143
Tēpora 143
Timna 156
Tirzah 18, 141, 156
Tryphena 141
Tryphosa 141

**U**

Unihi 143
Unknown Wife 29
Uriah's wife 141

**V**

Vashti 25, 26, 37, 64, 65, 66, 67, 68,
    140, 141, 153, 154

**W**

Wade, Mrs 133, 134
Washington, Martha 147

Watts, Naomi 147
Wesley, Anne (Nancy) 121, 125
Wesley, Emilia (Emily) 121, 122,
    123, 124, 125
Wesley, Keziah (Kezzy) 122, 124,
    125, 146
Wesley, Martha (Patty) 122, 124,
    125
Wesley, Mary (Molly) 121, 124
Wesley, Mary (mother of Samuel)
    121
Wesley, Mehetabel (Hetty) 121, 124,
    125, 147
Wesley, Susanna 114, 119, 122, 123,
    125, 148
Wesley, Susanna (Sukey) 121, 123,
    124, 125
White, Priscilla 147
Wilding, Cora 127
Williams, Esther 145
Williams, Marianne 133
Wise Woman 141
Wollstonecraft, Mary 147
Woman at the Synagogue 88, 106
Woman of the Streets 88, 108

**Z**

Zarephath, Widow of 141
Zebidah 139, 141
Zeresh 141, 152
Zeruah 136, 139
Zibiah 136, 138, 139
Zillah 141, 155
Zilpah 95, 141, 156
Zipporah 15, 141, 152, 156, 164

## Handy References for Special Occasions

| | | |
|---|---|---|
| Palm Sunday: | Woman of the streets | page 108 |
| Easter: | Joanna | page 110 |
| Mother's Day: | Hagar; Hannah | page 89; page 19 |
| Pentecost: | Sophia | page 12 |
| Queen's Birthday: | Esther | page 25 |
| Disability Sunday: | A Woman at the Synagogue | page 106 |
| Bible Sunday | Eunice | page 34 |
| Peace Sunday: | Achsah; Abigail | page 49; page 22 |
| Social Justice | Mahlah & Sisters | page 17 |
| Advent | Elizabeth; Anna | page 103; page 105 |

**Prayers for**

| | |
|---|---|
| Advent | page 160 |
| Disability Sunday | page 176 |
| Garden Blessing | page 111 |
| House Blessing | page 175 |
| Inclusiveness | page 108 |
| Intercession | page 162; page 163 |
| Mother's Day | page 167 |
| Simple pleasures | page 180 |
| Teamwork | page 32 |

**Poems about**

| | |
|---|---|
| A Winter's Day Retreat | page 170 |
| An Acrostic Psalm | page 169 |
| Easter Leaves | page 165 |
| Kapiti Island – A Prayer for Simple Pleasures | page 180 |
| Palms for Holy Week | page 166 |
| Sophia | page 12 |
| Where is Wisdom? | page 183 |

**Dialogues and Short Plays**

| | |
|---|---|
| Mahlah and Sisters: | page 17 |
| Rahab and Zada: | page 43 |
| Wife of Manoah: | page 54 |
| Hagar: | page 89 |
| Eve and the Snake: | page 38 |

# About the Author

Rosalie Reynolds Sugrue is a fifth generation West Coaster. Both her parents being fourth generation Coasters whose forebears came seeking gold. Rosalie's great grandfather, James Reynolds, was a local preacher from Cornwall who preached to miners on the beaches and helped establish the first Methodist church in Hokitika. His wife, Eliza, signed the petition that gave women the vote.

Rosalie's mother Elva Reynolds was a Methodist Deacon and also a lay preacher. Rosalie is a past president of the NZ Lay Preachers' Association, and the inaugural facilitator of the Methodist Lay Preachers Network 2004, serving as a co-facilitator until 2008. She has led hundreds of church services in New Zealand and the UK. She has also led rest home services, family services, cafe style worship, house blessings and devotions in many other situations.

A wife, mother, grandmother, great grandmother and author now retired Rosalie has worked as a psychiatric nurse, teacher and motellier. She has been active in Jaycees, the Methodist Women's Fellowship, the Community of Women and Men in Church and Society, National Council of Women, the Churches' Agency on Social Issues, Victim Support and U3A. She continues an active role as a lay preacher leading one to three services every month in a variety of churches.

# Also by Rosalie Sugrue
## Published by Philip Garside Publishing Ltd

**Lay Preaching Basics:** *A Practical Guide to Leading Worship* **(2018):** Do you want to learn how to preach and lead worship, but don't know where to start? This practical guide by experienced Methodist Lay Preacher Rosalie Sugrue will get you going. (In Print & eBooks)

**Ten Plays:** *Short, easy dramas for churches* **(Updated 2018):** Lay preacher Rosalie Sugrue's short plays and meditations are ideal to present in church. They encourage us to engage with Bible and historical characters and explore important themes. Staging is simple. Few props or costumes are required.
(In Print & eBooks)

**Theme Scheme:** *Creative Ideas, Activities, Games, Puzzles, Plays, Quizzes* **(Updated 2018):** Offers you a wealth of creative ideas, activities, games, puzzles and quizzes to help plan, organise and lead your group's programmes. All are fun and practical, requiring minimal equipment, and time to prepare.
(In Print & eBooks)

**The League of Lilith**: *A thriller with soul. Written with her son Troy Sugrue* **(2013):** Sarai, a Biblical Studies lecturer, learns a terrible truth; a core knowledge she must impart to a successor. Will she choose society wife, Jen, or bondage and discipline prostitute Kat? An explosive novel with a dramatic climax. (eBooks)

**Greens and Greys (2015):** Journey with Molly Sinclair through her 1950s childhood on the West Coast, her move to Christchurch for teacher training, drama-filled OE in the UK and Europe, and as she returns to NZ in the mid-1960s. An engaging coming-of-age tale.
(In Print & eBooks)